Dr. Bob Mullan, previously a lecturer in Sociology at the University of East Anglia, Norwich, is now a Producer/Director of film documentaries. He has written a host of other non-fiction books which most recently includes **Perfect Partners?** (Boxtree, 1987).

GW00492885

Other books by Bob Mullan

Stevenage Ltd
Approaching Social Theory (with E. Cashmore)
Life As Laughter: following Bhagwan Shree Rajneesh
The Mating Trade
Sociologists on Sociology
Uninvited Guests (with L. Taylor)
Zoo Culture (with G. Marvin)
The Enid Blyton Story
Are Mothers Really Necessary?
Perfect Partners?

IN SEARCH OF LOVE

Bob Mullan

Sphere Books

A Sphere Book

First published in Great Britain by Sphere Books Ltd.
1990

Printed and bound in Great Britain by
Richard Clay Limited, Bungay, Suffolk

ISBN 0 7474 0778 9

Sphere Books Ltd
A Division of
Macdonald & Co (Publishers) Ltd
Orbit House
1 New Fetter Lane
London EC4A 1AR

A Member of Maxwell Macmillan Pergamon Publishing
Corporation

Contents

Love is the triumph of imagination
over intelligence.

H.L. MENCKEN

You are my only love. You have me
completely in your power. I *know*
and *feel* that if I am to write anything
fine and noble in the future I shall do
so only by listening at the doors of
your heart. I would like to go through
life side by side with you, telling you
more and more until we grew to be
one being together until the hour
should come for us to die.

JAMES JOYCE, letter to Nora, 1909

Introduction:
A Society of Couples

> Americans, who make more of marrying for love than any people, also break up more of their marriages. This is not as much a failure of love as it is the determination of people not to live without it.
>
> MORTON HUNT

As Frankie Goes to Hollywood, to name merely one set of songsmiths, testify, there is nothing quite like the 'Power of Love'. It may well not, in fact, be able to move mountains but, nonetheless, most of us believe that love can conquer most things. Love is seen to be *the* most meaningful thing we can experience in life. With the companionship it brings in its wake, love is indeed considered to be the hub of life. To love and be loved, is all that is required. 'You're all I need to get by', sang Marvin Gaye and Tammi Terrell. *So* strong, however, is love that it can lead us to a moment of madness or a life of crime if such 'love' or the object of such love so motivates us. And love is *always* viewed as possessing healing properties. Whether it is to mend a 'broken heart' or to overcome loneliness, love, it is believed, *will* find a way.

But what is this thing called love? The stuff of innumerable songs, dreams - indeed the central theme of our lives. And how do we find it or, more

1

practically, how do we find someone we can fall in love with, then love, and stay with? How indeed.

It is expected that all of us will one day fall in love and settle down. Hopefully 'for ever'. 'It is as natural as learning to walk'; this is the only conclusion we can reach, considering that none of us is ever given any help in these matters. We are taught how to cross the road and avoid the juggernaut, yet the even greater possibility of the human misery produced by faulty marital choice and subsequent divorce is tossed at us like a harmless toy.

In Search of Love does not pretend to supply all the answers to such questions as 'what precisely is love?' or 'how can we find love that will last for ever?' Neither does it deny that there is mystery attached to discovering love and our perfect partner. Of course such mystery exists. No one will ever explain why *exactly we choose each other. However In Search of Love* does provide *some* answers, does dispel some myths about relationships and offers good advice as to how to find long lasting companionship.

Indeed perhaps a more appropriate title for this book would be *In Search of a Partner* for in these pages are details of how we look at ourselves, our self-image, as it is sometimes put; what we claim we are looking for in potential relationships, possible partners; and how we attempt to make our companions life-long ones, rather than ships passing in the night. But the title *In Search of Love* is no accident. As we have already intimated it is this thing called *love* that motivates the majority of us to find a possible partner for life - someone who will help us find and experience happiness.

But *again*, what precisely is love? Can we always be certain we have really, truly found it, this time around? What is its relation to sexual attraction? Is

2

love that quality which remains when sexual attraction wears thin? Indeed perhaps it is only when such sexual attraction disappears that love develops? Quite simply it is the extreme uncertainty of all of this which makes the reality of relationships such a brittle and inconclusive one; and one so difficult to comprehend. It is hardly surprising that so many relationships which begin so well, full of the joys of spring and so very hopeful, later fail - often quite miserably and spectacularly; always with pain and sadness, sometimes with bitterness.

Nearly all of us marry. No surprise. And perhaps it's no surprise that more and more of us are nowadays into not our *second marriages but our third*. And how long will *they* last? Another mark on the marital map is the reality of adultery, once seen as sinful now an everyday occurrence. Similarly many, many individuals - and, importantly, not solely women - live terribly unhappy, unfulfilled lives, constantly experiencing a state of imprisonment with those who were once their 'loved ones'.

There are almost as many definitions of love as there are individuals on the planet. It is presumably true that we all experience the emotion a little differently from one another. Equally the feelings we have and the decisions we make about possible partners are varied. Otherwise we'd all choose the same persons time and time again.

A number of individuals clearly believe that love and sexual attraction are almost the same thing - certainly many males, and not only the youthful ones, appear to mistake infatuation for love with an alarming regularity. Some of us firmly and passionately believe in 'love at first sight', while others amongst us fall prey to the influence of current cultural stereotyped thinking which may not *in fact* be a good basis for our choice of partner. For example some women believe that a prospective partner truly *ought* to be taller than themselves despite the fact that such physical qualities really have exceedingly little to do with the success or otherwise of a relationship. Similarly, many women still appear to demand that the man be older than themselves, again despite the probability that such an age difference will extend the length of time of the woman's widowhood. At a more seemingly trivial level there are those individuals whose choices are initially based on nothing more than fashion - 'blondes are "in", redheads out'.

At the psychological level we may seek out someone in particular, an individual with specific features or qualities for reasons unbeknown to us. For instance *he* might well be the person to replace a father, while *she* could well be the ideal replacement for his long-lost and beloved mother. Because of this subconscious influence, there is often a gap between what we *really* want in a partner and in a relationship, and that which we actually end up with.

Our choice of partner, seemingly an individual decision - whether made on the spur of the moment, or thought out over time - is often partly determined by factors somewhat beyond our control, or at least beyond our immediate understanding. Indeed such understanding often only surfaces on the therapist's couch or in the solicitor's office when divorce rather than love is the prime topic of conversation.

It is no wonder then that relationships fail so often and that love evaporates so frequently, leaving us perplexed and disappointed. *In Search of Love* attempts to be an account of love, relationships and companionship based on reality, rather than fantasy.

The research for the book is based on the thoughts and feelings of over 60,000 ordinary men and women each answering approximately 200 questions. In

4

other words the suppliers of over *twelve million answers*.

'Ordinary men and women' equals what exactly? In this book they are representatives of a wide range of occupational classes, the major religions and a variety of marital statuses. They are heterosexual, as are the majority of living individuals. (Homosexuality, a time-honoured human choice of sexual, social and emotional preference, is, sadly, beyond the scope of this book.)

The individuals who comprise the raw material of this book are 'ordinary' in the sense that a major preoccupation - *the* major preoccupation, for many of them - is to find a partner, a companion, a relationship which will help them move through the tortuous pathway of life. For these individuals being part of a couple is both exceedingly normal and utterly desirable. Defeat of such an aim results in painful loneliness and social unacceptance - social stigma.

In these pages will be found individuals who are widowed, separated or divorced, while others are virgins both sexually and partner-wise. Some of these individuals - virgins or divorcees - have coherent, well thought-out beliefs and aims. Others do not. Some have learned well and constructively from previous painful encounters. Others have not. Some know precisely what they want and have the ability and motivation to achieve their goals. Others do not.

So what we have in *In Search of Love* is a compendium of coherent views and less so; lives of the divorced, the once-bitten-twice-shy - well almost, and the virgins; those who have learned from the lessons of the past and those who never, ever will. In other words - a tableau of life as it really is.

It is important to stress the belief that contained here are *normal* accounts of the search for love and companionship. People *are* different and often, indeed regularly, behave unusually or in a different way to what we expect or desire. But most of us agree on a number of things: that love and work are, or should be, the central fulfilling aspects of life; that children bring pain as well as pleasure, but are nonetheless to be cherished; and that love is difficult to define but has something to do with physical, sexual attraction on the one hand and something bordering on altruism on the other. This book is about such people.

There are, of course, those who are quite different. For example the world has individuals suffering from *de Cleramboult's syndrome*, experiencing paranoid delusions connected with jealousy and erotic ideas - the *fatal attraction* of Glenn Close, to me and you. And there are also 'sex addicts': one study of the American self-help group Sexaholics Anonymous, suggests that in that country alone there are 13 million sex addicts. On the other hand some individuals are dedicated to the practice of celibacy - or chastity, if you like; they earnestly believe in their right to say 'no', despite cultural pressure to behave differently. This book is *not* about such people. It is about me and you.

Part one of *In Search of Love* describes what people say they want in their relationships and what kind of people they desire to meet, while part two profiles people who have met and subsequently become 'a couple'. Finally, part three attempts to chart an uncertain future and offer some conclusions.

Let us end this brief introduction with another statistic, again culled from the USA. One researcher has estimated that 50 per cent of all American marriages that do *not* end in divorce are unhappy and that only 10 per cent achieve their full potential. At the same time, however, there is broad agreement that living in couples is part of human nature. This

6

suggests that there is something radically wrong in our relationships - perhaps in our expectations of them and the way in which we choose the partners who will share those relationships with us.

PART ONE: IN SEARCH OF WHAT?

Chapter One:
What we say we want

> An archaeologist is the best husband
> a woman can have; the older she
> gets, the more interested he is in her.
>
> Attributed to *both* WOODY ALLEN
> and DOROTHY PARKER.

The pressure placed upon us from our childhood years to become part of a couple is relentless and unforgiving. Little boys are encouraged to be fighters and protectors - to protect the weak girls from the advancing Daleks, while the little girls themselves play with their miniature kitchens. Then as we grow a little older we are subjected to a bombardment of love and sexual messages through our ears by courtesy of popular music, a medium of far more importance to the impressionable young than the wise words of the aged. If we're 'madly in love' we simply turn up the volume to Barry White's tribute 'Just the Way You Are', or Anita Baker's 'Sweet Love', while if we suspect someone's interest in us is on the wane we could seek solace, or even bathe in self-pity, with the help of Barbra Streisand's 'You Don't Bring Me Flowers'. And if we're still recovering from a relationship break-up and still want a good wallow, 'Funny How Love Is', the Fine Young Cannibals' ironic little tune is just the fit.

Then of course there is the romantic novel aimed at, but certainly not read exclusively by, women. This is the literary genre which is read in the same way as an old sweater is worn - comfortably and reassuringly. Undemanding on the brain, such books rather aim to raise our hopes and expectations that love will find a way. For the older readers they have the secondary function of bringing back memories of being young and in love.

Feminists (who in their efforts to make women equal are seen by some to 'put women first') have spearheaded the attack on such 'romantic novels' with their tales of handsome doctors and fawning (but quietly beautiful) nurses, of male heroes pulling women to them and kissing them strongly, and so on. Their adverse reaction to them is based on the argument and belief that such books eat away at individual women's positive self-image, desire for independence and autonomy, and instead, encourage them to see themselves as wives and lovers, and to see 'love' rather than 'career' as *the* aim in life. Subsequently there has been an alternative publishing programme. Books of stories for 'young feminists', for example, with titles along the lines of 'some day your prince *won't* come', or 'there's more to life than a man'.

But there is also, not surprisingly, a middle way, an attempt to escape the absurd promises inherent in pure romantic fiction while still retaining some optimism that love and relationships are truly worth pursuing. The publishing world itself has long recognized that there exists to be exploited a large middle market of intelligent, broadly feminist girls and women who resent having to suspend their political views for the sake of a good rollicking read, yet who are nonetheless addicted to the traditional blockbuster. Indeed there are clearly thousands of intelligent females in demanding jobs who go home at night and watch 'Dallas' or the latest televised Andrea Newman, or read something completely undemanding and relaxing. Quite like an anaesthetic.

To satisfy this reality came this middle way, in the shape of - to name but one example - Meredith Tax's 'Passionate Women', a novel which, although similar to a blockbuster, can additionally be a vehicle for all kinds of ideas about the world, politics, life and so on, and which possesses a serious undercurrent. Such women readers desire entertainment with their self-improvement, but minus the insults to their intelligence.

Some individuals buy the sales pitch for coupledom so completely, with such an emotional investment, that they feel compelled to stay in relationships, however harmful they may be. So far the focus has been on women, and a self-help therapy has been initiated - Co-Dependants Anonymous - for women who are seen to be suffering from an addiction to painful relationships: women who choose the wrong man and yet stay with him no matter how much it hurts. Co-Dependency is seen as a way of having our emotional needs met, of using people like a drug.

The initiator of this therapy is Robin Norwood, and her book 'Women Who Love Too Much' is of particular importance. In it she describes the characteristics typical of women who 'love too much':

- Typically they come from 'dysfunctional homes', in which *their* emotional needs were not met.

- Having received little real nurturing themselves, they attempt to fill this unmet need vicariously by becoming a care-giver, especially to men who appear, in some way, needy.

- Because they were never able to actually change their parent(s) into the warm, loving care-taker(s) they longed for, they respond deeply to the familiar type of emotionally unavailable

11

men whom they can again try to change, through their 'love'.

- Terrified of abandonment, such women will do almost anything to keep a relationship from dissolving.

- Almost nothing is too much trouble, takes too much time, or is too expensive if it will 'help' the men they are involved with.

- Accustomed to lack of love in personal relationships, they are quite willing to wait, hope and try harder to please.

- They are willing to take far *more* than 50 per cent of the responsibility, guilt, and blame in any relationship.

- Their self-esteem is critically low, and they profoundly believe that they in fact do not desire to be happy. Rather, they believe they must earn the right to enjoy life.

- Such women have a desperate need to control their men and their relationships, having experienced so little security in childhood. They conceal their efforts to control people and situations as 'being helpful'.

- Within a relationship they are far more in touch with their dream of how it could possibly be, than with the reality of their situation.

- They are addicted to men and to emotional pain.

- Such women may well be predisposed emotionally and often biochemically to becoming addicted to alcohol, drugs, and/or particular foods, especially sugary ones.

- By being drawn to people with problems that need fixing, or by being enmeshed in situations that are chaotic, uncertain and emotionally painful, they avoid focusing on their responsibilities to themselves.

- They may well possess a tendency towards episodes of depression, which they try to forestall through the excitement provided by an unstable relationship.

- Such women are not attracted to men who are kind, stable, reliable and interested in them. Rather, they find such 'nice' men boring.

Presumably many of us recognize much of what has just been described. We may well be victims of the condition ourselves, to a greater or lesser degree. If not directly affected ourselves, the pain of such liaisons is nonetheless quite apparent. It makes the process of partner-choice even more important to get right.

Basics

As we have discussed, individuals make their choice of partner based on various considerations but are also affected by unconscious or partly-unconscious cultural or psychological factors. As *Women Who Love Too Much* graphically points out, many of us choose partners unwittingly in the belief that they may be able to replace a long-lost parent, one who did not give us the love we wanted and felt we deserved.

When it comes to considering cultural stereotyping which may well steer us into relationships which *really* aren't what we need or desire, we are often less than serious. We believe *others* are affected by them, but not us.

All stereotypes are *partial* descriptions of things, are *partial* truths. In the consideration of partner-choice there exists two sets of stereotyped beliefs, those concerned with what men and women are believed to want or desire and those desired by individuals themselves. It is asserted that what women want is *complex*: the list is - in no particular order - passion, commitment, independence, security, excitement, tenderness, stimulation, mutual support. On the other hand it is usually argued that what men want is simple, utterly fantastical, but simple, and while women may well stereotype the objects of their complex desires as caring hunks ('new men'?), gorgeous drongos or sexist meatheads, men characterize the objects of their more simple desires in terms of vamps, bimbos, blushing virgins, nymphettes and, of course, mythic mothers.

Pared down to *basics*, we all intuitively believe that men concentrate more on a potential partner's *physical* attributes, while women pay more attention to emotional qualities. This is not to say that men ignore such characteristics, or that women go out of their way to choose 'ugly' men if such men are emotionally sound. No, it is, rather, a matter of emphasis, or of degree.

In the pages that follow, we should learn more about what people seem to really want as well as what they *claim* they want. First, to basics.

Obviously it takes considerable time to *really* get to know someone, to understand what makes them tick, what hurts them and what gives them true pleasure, the events of the past that still leave their mark, the basis of their motivation, and so on. Many partners after years and years of marriage will be heard to say, 'we're still learning about each other even now!' Yet despite the existence of this process of getting to know someone over time, we nonetheless choose individuals who we claim will be 'partners for life' very quickly; indeed, often on the spur of the moment ('love at first sight'), usually after only a short period of time; and invariably a time free from real crises or dilemmas. And 'first impressions' have a tendency to last.

It sometimes seems as if Mother Nature herself is playing a game with the genders. For example men and women mature and peak sexually at quite different and often incompatible times. Moreover we are supposed to choose a partner for life *before* we've experienced those events in life which demonstrate whether or not the relationship is a fruitful one - financial crises, illness, parenthood.

Some individuals don't even get near the starting line. Before we actually meet and converse with our potential partners, we make all sorts of decisions about the kinds of people we are willing to consider, and those we are not. These basic predispositions colour everything else that follows. We may well rule out all smoking, small, manual working, Catholic, left-wing men or women before we even meet them. They are not even given a chance. *This* is how we make our choice.

So bearing in mind everything we have said about the power of stereotypes, and unconscious psychological factors playing a part in determining our choice of partner, whom in fact do we consider and whom do we exclude from consideration?

Our survey of ordinary people should enable us to understand some of the reasoning behind what, at times, appears to resemble more a battlefield than a marriage market.

Marital Status

The sample size of our survey is 68,041* - the equivalent of an average British town. Fifty-eight per cent of them are male, the rest female. Of the 68,041 almost 40 per cent of them are single men, while almost 19 per cent are single women. Interestingly

* See Appendix for details.

15

enough - and this is normal, taking the population as a whole - 67 per cent of this single category in the survey are men.

The next largest group is that of divorced people. In total, 27 per cent of the total survey are divorced, with more divorced women than men, 15 per cent as opposed to 12 per cent. Fifty-six per cent of divorced people in the survey are women.

The next category is that of the separated, comprising 9 per cent of the total. On this occasion there are more separated men than women, with 5 per cent of the total survey being separated men as opposed to the 4 per cent of separated women.In other words, 55 per cent of separated people in the survey are men.

The final category consists of the widowed, and 6 per cent of the total are represented by such people. Almost 4 per cent of the total survey are widows, and 2 per cent are widowers. There are then more widows than widowers, with 66 per cent of the widowed in the survey being widows.

The majority of people would like to find single partners, indeed 60 per cent of the total survey would like to meet people in this category. Very few of either sex reject the idea of finding a partner who is now, currently, single; although it has to be said that considerably more women than men do *not* want to meet prospective single partners (in the sample 1515 women, as opposed to 316 men). The explanation for this considerable difference, small in actual number, but significant in terms of meaning, is quite simple. Clearly women realize that relationships, perhaps unfortunately so, have a kind of trial-and-error quality; and that 'living with someone' is a considerable achievement of both compromise and learning how to deal with novel situations, novel challenges. So the logic behind those women who do *not* wish to meet single men, is that such men have not experienced such compromises or dilemmas, and have not had the opportunity to fail in a relationship and yet learn from them.

Additionally it is probably true that single men enter relationships with considerable naivete and/or misinformation, especially concerning women.There are some men who enter relationships with women, expecting the women to play the alternate roles of mother and sex-demon at their whim or fancy. Unless desperately thick-skinned or lacking a supply of brain cells, it will not take too long for most of these men to realize that most women don't actually play such games. But because of such male naivete it is perhaps a reason why some women do not want to meet single men - why should they spend potentially unfruitful and wasted years teaching their partners to grow up?

Finally women in general, let alone this minority who do not desire single men, are subjected to a cultural double standard which inevitably is bound to affect their judgement. This cultural idea specifies that a man should try to marry a virgin, after *he* has spent some years learning about sex - 'sowing his wild oats'. One need not be a Nobel prize winning mathematician to realize that in such a situation there is inevitably a shortfall of virgins, especially as there are more young males in the population than young females. Yet many males still cling to the dream, while many women realize the iniquity of the double standard and at the same time realize their true position in the course of things. In any event it is yet another reason why more women than men reject the idea of a prospective partner being single: they simply are not so brainwashed as males are to the idea of the virginal prize.

This is not to assert, of course, that women do not want to meet and marry single men - after all it is only a minority we are talking about. Indeed it could well

17

be argued that *more* women than men desire life-long attachments as women appear to understand more fully the commitments, responsibilities and emotional investment involved in them, and it is true that they tend to enter relationships with much hope in heart. We are not claiming that woman are *inevitably* the more reflective and intelligent sex; what we are simply suggesting is that women appear to be more *realistic* than men about the contours of relationships, especially after suffering an unsuccessful one.

Perhaps confirmation of the aforementioned is evident within the details of the next most 'wanted' category, namely of **divorced people**. Twenty-three per cent of the survey would *positively* like to meet them. Once again there are more women than men who would like to meet them; indeed nearly twice as many women as men would be prepared to engage in such an encounter (30 per cent as opposed to 18 per cent). Clearly, women appreciate the potential understanding and knowledge a divorced man might well possess following his failed marriage. But this is not to ignore the fact that 18 per cent of men *positively* want to meet divorced women; intuitively one knows that such a figure is also slowly on the increase, and not simply by virtue of an ever-escalating divorce rate, but also by the apparent desire of increasing numbers of men to enter into 'ready-made families'.

However, there is another point of view: almost 13 per cent of all the men in the survey do *not* want to meet divorced women, and almost 11 per cent of women turn their noses up at divorced men. This, of course, is hardly surprising. Despite the increasing divorce rate making marriage-divorce-marriage (and for some, another divorce and marriage) seem almost normal patterns of marital behaviour, many individuals cannot escape the notion of 'soiled goods'. An extension of the virgin bride/groom notion.

Perhaps realistically, such people do not wish to meet the divorced if it means meeting bitter or disenchanted persons. It is a situation riddled with confusions and dilemmas. Perhaps the reasoning goes something like this: 'Okay, this person must still have faith in relationships, must still be optimistic about love, or they wouldn't be prepared to meet me. However, perhaps it's a grudging optimism, perhaps a bitter realism, and perhaps their expectations are low, so low in fact that they might not put much into the relationship as they do not expect to get much out.'

What makes the matter even more complex is the fact that most of us are clearly aware that many people enter the fray once more for pragmatic reasons, such as those of finance and security. Reasons of survival, not of love and hope. Interestingly enough amongst the many unfolding future scenarios is one where we *all* divorce at some stage in our lives. If this interesting prospect ever did come to pass we would all have to juggle creatively the many contradictory emotions we'd possess; or simply become a society of cynics.

Another status often shrouded in issues of financial uncertainty and economic dependence, but which can also produce novel experiences relating to self-image, and matters of optimism and hope as opposed to the usual feelings of grief and despair, is that of **widowhood**. As Rudyard Kipling expressed it, exactly a century ago in 1890, widowhood is an unwelcome gift from nature:

> For a season this pain must endure
> For a little, little while
> I shall sigh more often than smile,
> Till Time shall work me a cure,
> And the pitiful days beguile.

In our survey almost 19 per cent of all individuals would be willing to meet the widowed. Of course the economic structure and dynamics of contemporary societies means that women are *usually* dependent on men, or if not, are usually treated economically in an unequal manner. And the traditional views on the women's role in child-rearing and the lack of alternative childcare facilities ensures that such an economic reality continues, for the time being, at any rate. So it comes as no surprise therefore that more women than men would be willing to meet the widowed, almost 28 per cent of women as opposed to 14 per cent of men.

Consider the implications here. Being prepared to meet and settle with someone who has *already* had, normally speaking, a long and happy married relationship, is a decision of considerable courage and maturity. We would have to develop a psychological outlook where we would not need constant reassurance that we were truly loved, while at the same time we would have to have that inner strength - for want of a better term - which prevented us from 'competing' with the deceased spouse. And at the same time we would need to be understanding and possibly forgiving on occasions, when we ourselves were placed in situations of competition by a partner unable to lose *their* memory of the deceased loved one completely.

So by virtue of the need to possess such a store of profound qualities it might come as no surprise that more women choose the path of accepting the widowed than men. Perhaps it is the challenge that invites; perhaps it is because, often, at these later ages there is less emphasis on matters sexual within relationships; perhaps there is even a degree of altruism, sadness and compassion involved, indeed perhaps the existence of something approaching a maternal love.

It would be unwise, however, to discount completely the pressures brought about by economic dependence that leads some women towards the widowed. Neither must we be blinkered about the 14 per cent of men also prepared to meet the widowed. Put simply, if somewhat cynically, there are gold-diggers amongst the male population as there are, no doubt, in the female world.

However it really would be wrong to contract the whole matter into one of economic need or exploitation. There *is* the fact of psychological challenge, there *is* the likelihood of entering a relationship less dependent on sexual performance than on compatibility, and there is no doubt the possibility that such a relationship might well help the single yet *fearful* individual who is desperately in need of an *experienced* companion - and certainly there are many stories of such contented couples.

Nonetheless, of our survey, 10 per cent of women do *not* want to meet widowers while almost 15 per cent of men do not want to meet widows. However, the widowed might be consoled to learn that they are not the *least* sought after group. That dubious honour falls to **separated people.** Only a total of 11 per cent of the survey definitely wish to meet them, with very slightly more men than women being prepared to meet people in this category.

The significance of such a statistic becomes clear when we consider that while 12 per cent of men do *not* want to meet separated women, over 36 per cent of women do *not* wish to encounter separated men. Put bluntly, the problem with the separated status is that it is so uncertain, so indeterminate. Is someone separated and therefore definitely to divorce eventually, or is a reconciliation possible? Certainly there are some people who are not taken seriously when they say they are separated. Women often take this description to mean that such men are in fact married but away from home, or unhappy at home, or desirous of appearing 'free' and single. In any event, alarm bells ring.

Physical attributes

In self-descriptions men and women in all the survey groups are fairly consistent in defining their physical attributes primarily as averagely attractive. For example, 85 per cent of men describe themselves as attractive, 10 per cent as not very attractive, while the remaining 5 per cent describe themselves as very attractive. The figures for women are comparable. There is nothing of any real surprise here. We certainly have to believe that we as individuals are reasonably presentable if we are going to successfully meet anyone in the current marital market. Nobody scores highly for either self-deprecation or timidity. What is required is a positive attitude and a sense of self-worth.

If there is any element of surprise at all in the statistics it is that so many individuals, 10 per cent from each sex, are prepared to describe themselves as 'not very attractive'. In contemporary western industrialized societies the *packaging* is everything. After all it is surely no exaggeration to argue that western culture, presently at least, is based on the appetite for *buying*, on the idea of a mutually favourable exchange. Buying is everything. Or as a piece of graffiti expounds, 'when the going gets tough, the tough go shopping'.

Therefore it is no surprise that, at one level at least, the relationship or marriage market follows similar rules, where 'attractive' partners are sought. 'Attractive' usually means a nice package of qualities which are popular and sought after on what we may call the personality market. Of course what specifically makes a person attractive depends on the fashion of the time, physically as well as psychologically. So pushing the analogy further, two persons 'fall in love' when they feel they have found the best object available on the market, bearing in mind the limitations of their own exchange values.

Perhaps the 10 per cent of each sex brave enough, or indeed truthful enough, to describe themselves as 'not very attractive' genuinely know that beauty *is* only skin deep and are consequently hoping for a relationship based on more enduring qualities; perhaps objectively they have inaccurately described themselves; perhaps someone will in fact see them as attractive, even 'very attractive'; perhaps they are willing to remain single.

In terms of *build* once more both men and women follow the contours of the stereotypes they have been encouraged over the years to follow. While about half of each sex describe themselves as being of 'average build', over 35 per cent of women describe themselves as 'slim' as opposed to 27 per cent of men, and similarly while only 10 per cent of women describe themselves as 'well built' over 17 per cent of men do so.

Being brainwashed by stereotypes helps us produce such a set of answers and is partly responsible for our concern with the 'body' which is possibly unparalleled in human history. Thousands of individuals all over the western world visit the gym to keep their bodies trim and in condition, some of them even visiting a clinic, therapist or doctor to discuss the reason why they need to visit the gym so often! And of course there are the so-called 'eating disorders' - 'so-called', because in reality they are disorders of the individual human personality and of an oppressive society. Certainly western societies seem determined to make us either extremely *slim* or extremely neurotic; sometimes leading us close to death.

Let us consider for example the phenomenon of anorexia nervosa, the principal symptoms of which include the rejection of food, cessation of menstrual periods in women, extreme and often dangerous forms of dieting and an obsessive fear of being overweight which frequently involves an apparent distortion of the individual's image of his or her body, imagining obesity in that extremely emaciated frame. It is on the surface a dietary condition, which has now become quite common, especially amongst female adolescents in the western world - although it is certainly not a condition exclusive to either females or adolescents. Indeed the rise of the neurotic, eating disordered adolescent male is a more recent phenomenon.

Therefore the fact that 35 per cent of the women describe themselves as 'slim' comes as no surprise. It is important for the partner-seeking female to both 'think thin' as well as attempt to be thin. A positive psychological self-image is often a prerequisite to real *actual* change.

The 17 per cent of men who describe themselves as 'well-built' are also not fearful of saying so. For a few decades now one of the prevailing stereotypes for males to live by has been that of the beefcake: the sturdy masculine physique. So, not surprisingly, a number of men are quite happy to see themselves in that way. The beefcake does not appeal to everyone, of course, as the rise of the aforementioned anorexic male adolescent testifies.

So what kinds of people do we wish to meet, in the somewhat basic terms of physical attraction?

About 60 per cent of both men and women claim that they would like to meet 'average' persons - in other words people like themselves. There is a degree of reason in this of course, but there is also the additional pressure of *decorum*. Of what is right.

'How can a reasonable person not want an ordinary, average person like me?', or words to that effect. Only a tiny minority of both sexes (only 4 per cent) positively desire to meet '*not* very attractive' persons.

If we pursue the matter further, we encounter yet another example of the male more than the female predispositioned to be interested in physical or sexual attraction; or as the Polish proverb puts it, 'love enters a man through his eyes; woman through her ears'.

There is no particular reason why partner-selection made *primarily* on the basis of physical attraction should be especially successful. 'Beauty' wears thin over time. Besides, the qualities necessary to develop and sustain relationships, and to overcome crises in life, are not likely to be evident from an individual's physical characteristics. Yet many of us - both men and women - continue to be attracted by the flimsiest of physical characteristics. Both sexes have fallen prey to the Hollywood scenario whereby worth and value in life tend to be equated with 'beauty'. Indeed people who are considered to be beautiful or positively attractive are treated more favourably by us all. Numerous industries, such as cosmetics, fashion, popular music and cinema encourage this behaviour. Men appear more prone to such messages. Whereas over 40 per cent of men would like to meet 'slim' women, only 28 per cent of women positively desire to meet 'slim men'. Finally, if any further proof is required, while over 25 per cent of women would actually positively like to meet 'well-built' men, only 8 per cent of men would positively like to meet 'well-built' women.

To conclude: although most of us appear to be looking for 'average lookers', when we examine our predeliction more closely we appear quite clearly to favour the prevailing and obviously persuasive stereotypes - slim very attractive women or, to a lesser extent, slim very attractive men.

None of this would matter if it were not for the degree of human misery and social fallout that unsuccessful relationships create. And let us not forget that the *majority* of divorces are initiated by women - the same women chosen in much earlier days by their men.

We have strenuously argued that stereotypes guide many of our thoughts and beliefs: and we are often unaware of such a fact. Unconsciously we may be led by the hand of the stereotype. Some stereotype behaviours may be actually quite logical and reasonable. Others less so. Take the following cases: the stereotype belief is that men prefer smaller women than themselves while women prefer taller men; similarly that men prefer younger women, while women in turn prefer older men. Implicit in this stereotyping is the notion that we *ought* to prefer such smaller/taller, younger/older people; that it somehow makes sense; and that it has always been that way.

Of course such stereotyping is senseless. Why on earth should women prefer taller men? Why should a smaller woman be more compatible than one taller? And why should a man really prefer a young woman, especially as the chances are that he will die before her in older age and leave her alone and widowed? Apart from a sexist answer that younger women are 'more attractive', there is no rational reply.

However our survey fell precisely in line with such stereotyped ideas. Indeed it is instructive to describe the findings in some detail in order to demonstrate the 'power of the stereotype'.

Thirty-two per cent of men are willing to meet women below 4' 8"; and 33 per cent of men are willing to meet women between 4' 8" and 4' 10"; 66 per cent of men are willing to meet women between 4' 10" and 5' 0"; 60 per cent of men are willing to meet women between 5' 0" and 5' 8"; 62 per cent of men are willing to meet women between 5' 8" and 5' 10"; 82 per cent of men are willing to meet women between 5' 10" and 6' 0"; 32 per cent of men are willing to meet women between 6' 0" and 6' 4"; 32 per cent of men are willing to meet women over 6' 4".

The most popular heights men are looking for in women are between 4' 10" and 5' 8". At the two extremes on the other hand there are fewer men looking for short or extremely tall women *but*, and it is an important *but,* the largest single category is that of 82 per cent wishing to meet 5' 10" and 6' 0" women. **It is significant that the largest number of men want to meet tall women.** We suspect that they expect them to be slim also, and so we have before us a stereotype.

These figures can be examined from a different viewpoint:

Hardly any men are 5' 0" or under, but 66 per cent of men are willing to meet women of that height. Similarly hardly any men are between 5' 0" and 5' 2" but 60 per cent of men are willing to meet women of that height. Only a total of 17 per cent of men are between 5' 4" and 5' 6" yet 60 per cent of men are nonetheless willing to meet women of that height. Similarly 13 per cent of men are between 5' 6" and 5' 8" but 60 per cent of men are willing to meet women of that height. Twenty-seven per cent of men are between 5' 8" and 5' 10" but 62 per cent of men are willing to meet women of this height. Only 26 per cent of men are between 5' 10" and 6' 0" yet 82 per cent of men are willing to meet women of this height. Eleven per cent of men are between 6' 0" and 6' 2" but 30 per cent of men are willing to meet women of this height. Three per cent of men are between 6' 2" and 6' 4" yet 32 per cent of men are willing to meet women of such a height. Only a handful of men are 6' 4" plus yet 32 per cent of men are willing to meet such tall women.

The significance of these statistics are evident when compared with those of women.

Six per cent of women want men under 4' 8"; 6 per cent of women want men between 4' 8" and 4' 10"; 21 per cent of women want men between 4' 10" and 5' 0"; 21 per cent of women want men between 5' 0" - 5' 8"; 25 per cent of women want men between 5' 8" and 5' 10"; 96 per cent of women want men between 5' 10" and 6' 0"; 78 per cent of women want men between 6' 0" and 6' 4"; 78 per cent of women want men over 6' 4".

If we look at the range 5' 0" to 5' 8" for both men and women, we can see that this average is being looked for by only 21 per cent of women whereas there are 60 per cent of men looking for a similar average. Also if we look at the figures either side of this average we see that whereas 33 per cent of men are willing to accept 4'8" to 4' 10" women, only 6 per cent of women want men of this same height. At the lowest height, whereas 32 per cent of men are willing to accept women below 4' 8" only 6 per cent of women are interested in men of this height. So whereas many men are willing to accept shorter women, women are certainly not looking for short men. It is however still important to bear in mind that the two largest percentages of men are looking for women between 5' 8" and 5' 10" and 5' 10" and 6' 0".

We pointed out that the single largest category was that of men looking for 5' 10" to 6' 0" women; the same indeed is the case for women but the percentage is even greater. While 82 per cent of men are willing to meet women of this height, 96 per cent of women are willing to meet men of this height. Interesting comparisons can also be made at the very top of the scale. Extremely tall women are quite popular with men - some 32 per cent of men are willing to meet women between 6' 0" and 6'4", and over, but just over 78 per cent of women are willing to meet men of that height. So whereas very tall women are reasonably acceptable for men, **very tall men are highly desired by women.**

Another way of expressing the 'heights requirement' of women is as follows:

Hardly any women are under 4' 10" but 6 per cent of women want to meet men of this height; 5 per cent of women are between 4' 10" and 5' 0" but 21 per cent of women are willing to meet men of this height; 17 per cent of women are between 5' 0" and 5' 2" and 21 per cent of women are willing to meet men of this height; 27 per cent of women are between 5' 2" and 5' 4" but *only* 21 per cent of women are willing to meet men of this height; 36 per cent of women are between 5' 4" and 5' 6" but *only* 21 per cent of women are willing to meet men of this height; 7 per cent of women are between 5'6" and 5' 8" whereas 21 per cent of women are willing to meet men of this height; 5 per cent of women are between 5' 8" and 5' 10" yet 25 per cent of women are willing to meet men of this height; only 2 per cent of women are between 5' 10" and 6' 0" yet 96 per cent of all women are willing to meet men of this height; hardly any women are between 6' 0" and 6' 2" but 78 per cent of all women are willing to meet men of this height. No woman in the survey is 6' 2" - 6' 4" yet 78 per cent of all women are willing to meet men of this height. No woman is 6' 4" plus yet 77 per cent of all women are willing to meet men of this height.

This shows very clearly that women are looking for men *much* taller than themselves. They obviously do not want to be with short men.

If we turn to *age*, our first set of statistics refer to the requirements expressed by men: 41 per cent of men are willing to meet women under 20 years. Eighty per cent of men are willing and desire to meet women between 21 and 30 years. Seventy-four per cent of men are willing to meet women between 31 and 40 years. Twenty-nine per cent of men are prepared to meet women between 41 and 50 years. Only 8 per cent of men are willing to meet women between 51 and 60 years. Once more, expressed somewhat differently, the statistics add up in the following manner:

Only 4 per cent of men are under 20 yet 41 per cent of men are willing to meet women of that age. Thirty-eight per cent of men are between 21 and 30 yet 80 per cent of men are willing to meet women of that age. Thirty four per cent of men are between 31 and 40 but 74 per cent of men are nonetheless willing to meet women of that age. Seventeen per cent of men are between 41 and 50 but 28 per cent of men are willing to meet women of that age. Six per cent of men are between 51 and 60 but a mere 8 per cent of men are willing to meet women of that same age.

If we turn to women the comparable figures are as follows:

Five per cent of women are willing to meet men under 20 years. Thirty per cent of women are willing to meet men between 21 and 30 years. Sixty per cent of women are willing to meet men between 31 and 40 years. Sixty-three per cent of women are willing to meet men between 41 and 50 years. Forty per cent of women are willing to meet men between 51 and 60 years.

Once more expressed differently:

Five per cent of women are under 20 and only 5 per cent of women are willing to meet the same aged men. Only 18 per cent of women are between 21 and

30 but 30 per cent of women are willing to meet men of this same age. Only 31 per cent of women are between 31 and 40 yet 60 per cent of women are willing to meet men of this age. Only 30 per cent of women are between 41 and 50 yet again 63 per cent of women are willing to meet men of this same age. Only 13 per cent of women are 51 to 60 yet 40 per cent of women are willing to meet men of this age.

So women are, *on average*, looking for men who are older than themselves. If this is compared with the percentages for men we notice important contrasts. While 80 per cent of men are willing to meet 21 to 30-year-old women only 30 per cent of women are interested in men of this age. While 74 per cent of men are willing to meet women of 31 to 40 only 60 per cent of women are interested in men of this age. The percentages then swing around with the cases of older men and women. While only 29 per cent of men are willing to meet women between 41 and 50 years, a total of 63 per cent of such women are willing to meet men of this age. Finally only 8 per cent of men are willing to meet women in the oldest group of 51 to 60 years, yet 40 per cent of women are willing to meet these older men.

Clearly the persuasive power of stereotypes is at work here in the cases of both height and age requirements requested.

Habits

When relationships begin to go wrong it is often evident from the everyday fabric of life. Behaviour which was once tolerated, even encouraged, by one partner soon becomes undesirable or an irritant. Earlier compromises are forgotten. Our partners' habits, once part of their personalities, become unacceptable. How often have we heard people say that it is indeed the little things that count. So what

31

do we know about the habits that *initially* attract or repel us?

Of our survey, in keeping with national trends, non-smokers are much in evidence. Seventy per cent are non-smokers, with more male non-smokers (40 per cent) than female non-smokers (30 per cent). This is once more in keeping with national trends and is not only a worrying trend, but also partly due to an advertising campaign dedicated to increase the number of young smoking women.

Despite this, both men and women are extremely strong on wanting partners who do not smoke *at all* - over 50 per cent of men and almost the same amount of women. Clearly there must be many women who do not approve of their own smoking - perhaps they feel that by meeting a non-smoker they themselves might stop. Very few people positively desire a meeting with smokers - only 8 per cent of men and 9 per cent of women.

If smoking appears to be the current bogeyman, in terms of socially acceptable or desirable behaviour, drinking appears to be less of a problem. Most people in our survey do not wish to define themselves as non-drinkers. Indeed only 4 per cent of the total - and slightly more men than women - define themselves in such a way. However 'regular drinking' is not such a popular definition either, only 17 per cent of the total survey. Once again individuals are defining themselves in what they consider to be socially acceptable terms: it is unacceptable either to drink nothing or drink regularly.

Therefore it comes as no great surprise that the majority of people - over 78 per cent - describe themselves as 'occasional drinkers'. More specifically 75 per cent of men do so, as opposed to the slightly greater 82 per cent of women.

The *desired* individual, for both men and women in the survey, is the 'occasional drinker'. Over half of all men and women are positively happy to meet such a person, 50 per cent of women, 46 per cent of men. Again the slight effect of the stereotype: it is considered more acceptable for the male to drink.

Approximately 11 per cent of men are willing to meet women who define themselves as 'regular drinkers', with the comparable figures for women being the slightly less one of 10 per cent. Given that there are fewer women in the survey than men, it does seem therefore that it is indeed more acceptable for a man to be a regular drinker than a woman.

Not surprisingly only 10 per cent of men positively want to meet 'non-drinking' women, while only 9 per cent of women desire to meet 'non-drinking' men. This, of course, could well be seen as an act of compromise, of mental juggling. For as most of us know, the consumption of alcohol does very little of a positive nature towards the fruitfulness of relationships. What results is often merely a touch of Dutch courage (also known as, 'being blind to reality'), poor sexual performance and, most distressingly, a disruption of financial security and a tendency toward aggression or poor communication. *Yet*, in spite of all this, we feel obliged to accept a drinking partner within a relationship, while we keep fingers crossed. Additionally there lingers another stereotyped belief, *viz* that there is something slightly wrong or eccentric with a man who does not drink.

Further statistics confirm the aforementioned: only 11 per cent of men don't want to meet women who 'don't drink' at all, while even more women - 15 per cent - don't want to meet men who are absolute non-drinkers. Finally, a glimpse of sanity: 16 per cent of men do not want to meet women who define themselves as 'regular drinkers', while over 25 per cent of women reject 'regular drinking' men.

We are not engaged here in a campaign against drinking. We merely acknowledge the reality that within emotionally and sexually fired relationships, alcohol consumption does not encourage rational, dispassionate communication between fraught or misunderstood partners. On the contrary, it often acts in such a way as to bring out the worst rather than the best in individuals. Things best not said become spoken, and behaviour can change dramatically - witness the accounts of domestic violence. And for the economically deprived, often a disproportionate amount of their shrunken budget can be consumed by alcohol. 'If there is nothing else in life, why not?', may well be the understandable refrain.

Religion, education and politics

If smoke *does* get in your eyes, if waking up next to someone stinking of alcohol turns you off, if it irritates you that your partner squeezes the toothpaste from the wrong end, how will you react when it comes to the larger issues and distinctions that could cause conflict in a relationship? The religion we belong to, the religions we reject? Our educational backgrounds, achievements? Whom we vote for?

The large percentage in the survey are those who define themselves, unsurprisingly, as Church of England. Over 55 per cent of the survey did so, 52 per cent of whom were men, 47 per cent women. Perhaps a little more surprisingly is the category of 'no religion'; indeed a total of 30 per cent employed *this* self-definition. Three-quarters of this 30 per cent were men, the remainder women. Many more men than women in the survey define themselves as having 'no religion' - 36 per cent of *all* men, as opposed to 23 per cent of *all* women.

A small proportion of the survey are Roman Catholics - 3 per cent - while an even smaller minority are Islamic. Less than 1 per cent of the survey holds a belief in atheism: a positive rejection of the religious view of life. Finally the smallest category is that of the Jewish religion, with again less than 1 per cent.

Such statistics reflect national - and historical - trends: there *has* been a steady decline over the last few decades in church attendance - usually taken as the definition of religious belief, and affiliation; and it is generally believed that women are more likely to be religious than men. Certainly, more young males than females have been encouraged to embrace scientific perspectives; and religious and spiritual sentiment has been seen as more fitting for the 'emotional' needs of women in the past. Perhaps a related explanation of the tendency of women to become more 'spiritually' religious than the men, is that perhaps women have to suffer more in life - biological crises, the burden of chief parenting, being married - and therefore have more of a need to turn towards their God. (On the other hand some men might look upon religious fervour as being a less than masculine emotion.)

In terms of *wants*, the highest percentage in the survey were those who positively wished to meet Church of England people - 31 per cent in total expressed such a wish, of which a greater proportion were women. Less than 1 per cent of both sexes positively stated that they did *not* want to meet someone from the Church of England.

Following surprisingly quite closely behind were the 24 per cent of the survey who positively wished to meet people holding 'no religion'. Slightly more men than women expressed such a desire (25 per cent of men, 21 per cent of women). In terms of *not* wishing to meet individuals holding 'no religion' only 2 per cent of men expressed such a point of view, with only about twice as many women expressing this. In other words, despite the small percentages, nonetheless there is a much higher percentage of women rejecting non-religious men.

About 12 per cent of the total survey positively claimed that they would be willing to meet Roman Catholics - slightly more women than men. Conversely, approximately 10 per cent of men said that they did *not* wish to meet Roman Catholic women, while 14 per cent of women said they did *not* want to meet Roman Catholic men.

Despite the constant claim we, as a nation, make that ours is a pluralistic, integrative and cosmopolitan society it is clear that our minorities are well-defined, demarcated and perceived as being different from the mainstream. For example while in total 4 per cent of the survey would be willing to meet Jewish people, over 32 per cent of men stated categorically that they did not want to meet Jewish women while over 41 per cent of women similarly had no desire to meet Jewish men.

A similar set of figures arise from a consideration of atheism. About 5 per cent would be willing to meet atheists - men and women - but over 50 per cent of men do not want to meet female atheists, while an even greater 70 per cent of women do not want to meet atheistic men. We have already argued that it is likely that more women have an affinity for religion than men, and the previous statistic bears this out.

Less than 1 per cent of the survey wish to meet Muslims, possibly the most misunderstood religious grouping of all.

Slightly more men than women would be prepared to meet someone from the Islamic faith. Similarly, while 21 per cent of men positively do *not* want to meet Muslims, even more women - 33 per cent - express this disinclination towards Muslim men. Again these are hardly surprising figures, especially when we consider the widespread publicity - not always accurate - given to the position of women within Islam.

So, in summary, the greatest *rejection* rate is of atheists. It appears that we prefer *any* religion to those individuals who have an extremely negative attitude to it or who reject the idea of religion altogether.

In keeping with a modern, predominantly literate nation, our survey consists of a majority of individuals holding some sort of educational qualification. Indeed in total only 15 per cent of the people in the survey possess no educational qualifications whatsoever.

At the level of qualifications obtained at school the women in our survey are slightly higher achievers. However there is a quite massive difference when it comes to *technical qualifications* - 22 per cent of the men have such qualifications, as opposed to less than 1 per cent of women: merely confirmation that the professional market does not embrace women so readily as men, plus the more insidious fact that in the not so distant past women have been trained from childhood to accept marital roles rather than career roles. As Emma Goldman, in *Marriage and Love*, somewhat caustically puts it: 'From infancy, almost, the average girl is told that marriage is her ultimate goal; therefore her training and education must be directed towards that end. Like the mute beast fattened for slaughter, she is prepared for that.'

Our women are also a little behind men in terms of *university qualifications* - 29 per cent of men and only 24 per cent of women.

Interestingly enough, yet - dare we say it - hardly surprising, is that when we look at what our men and women are seeking a familiar pattern emerges: while over 41 per cent of women would positively like to meet a man in possession of a higher qualification, only 21 per cent of men are in search of women with such qualifications. Even in terms of those qualifications obtained at school, women are more interested in meeting men with them, as opposed to men who can happily live with women who do not have them. And whereas 11 per cent of men would accept women with no qualifications whatsoever, only 6 per cent of women positively wanted to meet men devoid of qualifications.

Significantly women have a higher percentage in the *rejection* of men with no educational qualifications - almost half of them (49 per cent) did not wish to meet such uneducated men, but only 24 per cent of men rejected women with no educational qualifications. Finally while only 4 per cent of women did *not* wish to meet university educated men, significantly 8 per cent of men - twice as many as the women - did *not* want to meet women educated to university level.

In other words: intuitively we feel confident that the aforementioned statistics are further proof that men continue to be led by stereotypes and their upbringing. They appear not to be too bothered by the educational status of the women they hope to meet.

It is indeed hard, given the earlier evidence, to resist the cynical conclusions that women need no particular qualifications to perform their roles as sex slave, domestic servant and mother. Similarly, the greater desire on the part of women to meet educationally qualified - and therefore, hopefully, 'intelligent' - men, appears to be in line with other findings, most notably that they are less interested than men in the outward and superficial qualities, like physical appearance, of their prospective partners.

In the middle of many domestic and social disputes we are often informed by the nearest sage that 'we should never argue about politics ... we can never agree, on such things, **In matters of love, do politics count?**

Of those people in the survey who make a positive statement about politics the largest group is the 'centre group'. They number 38 per cent of the survey. Such a figure represents social respectability and is quite predictable: as with all those people who describe themselves as 'average', similarly most of us like to be seen as in the centre of politics. Safe, respectable and predictable. And of course the major political parties of the modern western societies are of the centre. So the next set of figures are equally predictable: those who define themselves as right wing make up 13 per cent of the total, while those who see themselves as left wing amount to a total of 6 per cent of the survey. This actually leaves 'not interested in politics' as the largest single category - 42 per cent of the total - a great irony coming as it does from one of the homelands of democracy. Such a figure means a number of things, taken to a national level: that democracy *does* mean the right to be *dis*interested as well as enthusiastic about politics and power; that basically, given the predominance of both disinterested and centrist people, very little really changes in the realm of politics and law; that there is a considerable fear of so-called extreme groups, especially those situated on the left.

Taking women separately, over 46 per cent claim to be disinterested in politics, while 35 per cent see themselves as in the centre, 13 per cent on the right, 6 per cent on the left. The figures for men are almost identical, with just a few more in the centre and a few less disinterested individuals. But do politics matter when it comes to choosing a partner? Can a Militant supporter settle down with a Thatcherite? Can a cosy breakfast be shared between a Labour supporter and a Tory? Do democrats and republicans fall in love?

Quite frankly, the survey suggests that people are not *too* worried about the political views of their potential partners although, as we will see, they do reject certain groups.

If we begin with the centre grouping, only 29 per cent of men and 32 per cent of women say they *particularly* want to meet someone who is centre. Indeed 12 per cent of men are willing to meet those women 'not interested' in politics, while 11 per cent of centre women are prepared to meet 'not interested' men. Small percentages of centrist men and women - 5 per cent and 8 per cent - are prepared to meet those on the right wing. The least popular group for those in the centre are those on the left.

In terms of *definite rejection*, 18 per cent of centre men say they simply do not want to meet left-wing women, while the considerable total of over 23 per cent of centre women positively do not wish to meet left-wing men. Similarly right-wing individuals are rejected by centre people, albeit to a slightly lesser degree. Finally only 2 per cent of centre men and 5 per cent of centre women do *not* wish to meet the 'not interested'. It seems fair to say that few people have very definite views or beliefs, but that for most individuals political definitions of potential partners are not very important so long as they are not too definite - that is, they do not want 'lefties' and many of them equally do not want right-wingers. Instead they want to meet those people they believe to be 'normal' people.

Focusing solely on the right-wingers, 30 per cent of right-wing men and 40 per cent of right-wing women would like to meet right-wingers of the opposite sex. Hardly a surprising statistic given the unpopularity of holding right-wing views: no wonder they want to meet some of their own kind. However, in keeping with our earlier observation that politics isn't *that* important in the search for a partner, some right-wing individuals are prepared to meet people of other political persuasions. For example 12 per cent of right-wing men and 11 per cent of right-wing women are prepared to meet the politically 'not interested'. However only 2 per cent of right-wing men positively wish to meet left-wing women, with a similar figure for right-wing women. The actual *rejection* rate of other political types by the right-wing is significant if not surprising. Specifically over 42 per cent of right-wing men simply do *not* wish to be introduced to females on the left, while 52 per cent of right-wing women have no wish to meet men of the left. Only 1 per cent of right-wing men do not want to meet centre women, while a mere 2 per cent of right-wing women do not wish to meet men of the centre. Similar figures apply to the potential meeting of the 'not interested'.

Finally, another unpopular group in the political section of the survey, the left-wing people. This group is somewhat more definite in wanting to meet people of their own political persuasion, with 40 per cent of such men and 45 per cent of left-wing women wishing to meet fellow left-wingers. Once more, this is hardly surprising, given that of all the political persuasions individuals on the left make much less of a distinction between the personal and political life: hence the left's concern with issues such as domestic violence, and freedom in sexual lifestyles. It seems that it would be rather difficult for someone on the left to share a marital bed with someone of contrary political beliefs.

However, as a reflection of their belief that they are reasonable people, 14 per cent of left-wing men and 15 per cent of left-wing women are prepared to meet people of the centre. There are similar figures for meeting the 'not interested', perhaps surprising given the left's firm belief in the importance of politics.

There do exist some masochists, however: 3 per cent of left-wing men and 3 per cent of left-wing women are prepared, indeed willing, to meet individuals on the right. Or perhaps this is a sign that the search for love comes before everything else.

Another thought on this small percentage of left-wing individuals who positively *wish* to meet those on the right wing, is that they welcome a challenge. Perhaps this would be the opportunity for conversion, the potential to change ballot-box behaviour.

In terms of pure *rejection*, it is hardly surprising that 42 per cent of left-wing men and, greater still, 56 per cent of left-wing women do *not* wish to meet people of the right. The next most rejected group are those 'not interested' in politics - rejected by 7 per cent of left-wing men and 14 per cent of left-wing women. Most of the left wing do not mind those in the centre.

It would appear that in general women are more clear than men about the sort of political person they wish to meet. They are, for example, more definite that they would like to meet men of their own political beliefs and also they reject more forcefully men who do *not* hold the same beliefs as themselves. Perhaps the explanation is that even if men do possess particular views, they do not care what their women think or that simply they are not so interested in finding a woman who shares them.

Racial types, racial stereotypes

We have looked at minority views and minority groups: Islamic, atheistic, Jewish, the left and right-wingers. If we put political groupings and political 'wants' in tandem with racial groupings, including minorities, there arise some interesting points. For example we might expect those on the political left to be more willing to meet 'foreigners', but this does not occur to any dramatic degree. The left-wingers are more willing than other groups to accept them but the percentages are not very high.

Most of us desire to meet Europeans - in terms of men, 75 per cent of the centre, 80 per cent from the right and 66 per cent from the left express a desire to meet European women. Women from those groups have similar percentage rates to those of the men wishing to meet European women.

Of the Europeans in the survey, only 3 per cent of centre men, 2 per cent of right-wing men and the slightly greater rate of 5 per cent of left-wing men want to meet women from Africa and the West Indies. The figures for women are comparable, albeit a little lower.

When we examine the statistics for *rejection* the pattern is even stronger.

Less than 1 per cent of centre men do not want to meet European women, 12 per cent do not want to meet Southern Europeans, (Spanish, Italian, Greek etc), 32 per cent do not want to meet Chinese or Japanese, 42 per cent do not wish to meet those of Middle Eastern origin, while 55 per cent do not want to meet Indian or Pakistani women.

Less than 1 per cent of centre women do not want to meet European men, 31 per cent do not wish to meet Southern European men, while 72 per cent do not want Chinese and Japanese men. Seventy per cent do not want Middle Eastern men, 77 per cent do not wish to meet Indian and Pakistani men and finally 76 per cent do not want African and West Indian men.

Of right-wing men, less than 1 per cent do not want European women, 17 per cent do not want Southern European women, while 38 per cent do not want Chinese and Japanese women. Fifty-one per cent do not want to meet Middle Eastern women, 65 per cent do not want Indian and Pakistani women and finally 70 per cent do not want to meet African and West Indian women.

Again, less than 1 per cent of right-wing women do not want to meet European men, 37 per cent do not want Southern European men, and then their rejection becomes quite powerful - 79 per cent do not want to meet Chinese and Japanese men, 77 per cent do not want Middle Eastern men, while 84 per cent do not want Indian and Pakistani men, and finally 84 per cent equally do not wish to meet African and West Indian men.

The rejection on the part of left-wing men is slightly less marked than the other groups, but still nonetheless follows the same pattern. Less than 1 per cent do not want European women, 7 per cent do not want Southern European women, while 21 per cent do not want to meet Chinese and Japanese women, and 27 per cent do not want Middle Eastern women. Finally, 34 per cent of them do not want to meet Indian and Pakistani women and 38 per cent do not want African and West Indian women.

The rejection rate by left-wing women is not as high as right-wing women, but again it follows more or less the same pattern (although they do not reject African men as much as they reject Chinese and Japanese men), and they have a higher percentage of rejection than the left-wing men. Less than 1 per cent do not want to meet Europeans, while 22 per cent do not want to meet Southern Europeans, and 57 per cent do not want to meet Chinese and Japanese men. Moreover, 55 per cent do not want to meet Middle Eastern men, 60 per cent do not want to meet Indian and Pakistani men and, finally, 53 per cent do not want to meet African and West Indian men.

So despite the fact that the left-wing group has a lower rejection rate than any other they still do *not* particularly want to meet foreigners. With, for example, a total of 66 per cent of left-wing men wishing to meet European women compared with a mere 5 per cent who want to meet African or West Indian women. Seventy-six per cent of left-wing women want to meet European men compared with only 5 per cent who want to meet African and West Indian men.

All in all the aforementioned clearly demonstrates that most of us live our lives both in a most conventional and low-risk manner, and moreover that we probably do not know much about other racial groups and do not wish to learn.

Let us examine the racial constitution of our own survey, and the lessons it may well teach us.

In *all* of the racial categories represented in the survey - with the exception of the Chinese and Japanese - there are many more men than women. For example there is a significant difference among the Europeans, as 58 per cent of all Europeans are men while 43 per cent are women - a 15 per cent difference. With the other racial groups the differences are even greater. For example, the next biggest category is the African and West Indian one where the breakdown is 55 per cent of men and 45 per cent of women, so the difference here is only 10 per cent. Then we have the Southern European category where there are a total of 64 per cent of men and 36 per cent of women - a difference of some 28 per cent. The Indian and Pakistani category shows that there are 73 per cent of men and 27 per cent of women, a difference of some 46 per cent. Then there follows the Chinese and Japanese with the only difference in terms of percentages of male/female - 47 per cent men and 53 per cent women - unusually a mere 5 per cent greater number of women. Finally comes the Middle Eastern category with 82 per cent of men and 18 per cent of women - a quite massive 64 per cent difference.

All these groups have a greater percentage of **single people** than the European group. Sixty-seven per cent of European men in the survey are single and 44 per cent of European women are single, while 83 per cent of African and West Indian men are single and 68 per cent of African and West Indian women are single and, finally, 70 per cent of Southern European men are single, with 49 per cent of Southern European women being single.

Seventy six per cent of Indian and Pakistani men are single, with 64 per cent of Indian and Pakistani women being also single, while 76 per cent of Middle Eastern men are single and 54 per cent of Middle Eastern women are single. Finally, 84 per cent of Chinese and Japanese men are single and 69 per cent of Chinese and Japanese women are single.

The next highest category for any of the groups is that of **divorced people:** 21 per cent of European men in the survey are divorced as are 37 per cent of European women, while 11 per cent of African and West Indian men are divorced and 21 per cent of African/West Indian women. There are a total of 21 per cent of South European divorced men in the survey, with 36 per cent of South European women also being divorced. Thirteen per cent of Indian and Pakistani men are divorced and 25 per cent of Indian and Pakistani women are divorced, while 16 per cent of Middle Eastern men are divorced and almost twice as many, 32 per cent, of Middle Eastern women are similarly divorced. Finally, 9 per cent of Chinese and Japanese men are divorced while there are 17 per cent of Chinese and Japanese divorced women.

So the majority of these people in our survey have either never been in a relationship which has ended in marriage, or they indeed have but it has ended in divorce.

The **separated category** is quite a small one: 8 per cent of European men and 9 per cent of European women in the survey are separated, while 6 per cent of African and West Indian men and 6 per cent of African and West Indian women are separated. A total of 7 per cent of South European men are separated, with the corresponding figure for South European women being 8 per cent. Nine per cent of Indian and Pakistani men are separated and 6 per cent of Indian and Pakistani women are separated, while 6 per cent of Middle Eastern men and 5 per cent of Middle Eastern women are separated. Finally a total of 7 per cent of Chinese and Japanese men are separated, while 9 per cent of Japanese and Chinese women are also separated.

The widow and widower category is really quite insignificant for all groups except for the Europeans. For example there are very few Chinese or Japanese widows or indeed Indian or Pakistani widows. Such bereaved individuals obviously do not bother to look for new wives or husbands, perhaps by virtue of the fact that they will be living within extended families and therefore do not feel the need to start a new relationship. Whereas, on the other hand, the European widowed people would probably be living on their own and therefore would desire another partner in an attempt to avoid loneliness.

If we look at what people say they want, in terms of racial types there are, not surprisingly, no great diversions from the low-risk pattern. While 78 per cent of European men are looking for European women, conversely 86 per cent of European women are willing to accept their European counterparts. The next most acceptable category is of the South European with 19 per cent of European men willing to accept women from this group and 13 per cent of

European women willing to accept South European men. However, there are still quite large numbers of European men willing to accept women from other groups: for example, 12 per cent would accept Chinese or Japanese women, 5 per cent would accept women from the Middle East, 4 per cent would accept Indian or Pakistani women, and finally 3 per cent would accept African and West African women. The reverse however is not true for European women: less than 1 per cent would accept Chinese or Japanese men, a mere 1 per cent would accept Middle Eastern men with a similar figure in respect of Indian or Pakistani men, while 1 per cent would accept African and West Indian men.

So the pattern is quite obvious with the vast majority wanting to find *white* partners. Perhaps the difference between the sexes is similarly quite predictable. We have already established the fact that men are more likely to choose a partner on the basis of their physical attributes than women would, and so perhaps there is the appeal of the exotic, a different colour to their own. This, of course, could be tied in with the belief many European men hold that non-European women - women from Thailand, Japan, the Philippines, for example - are more compliant, less inhibited sexually and, generally speaking, 'know their place'.

If we look at what the individuals in our survey would *not* accept there emerges a similar pattern. Very few **European** men - less than half a per cent - would *not* accept European women while, on the other hand, the *least* popular group is the African and West Indian women - rejected by a total of 61 per cent. Indian and Pakistani women are rejected by 58 per cent, then follow: Middle Eastern women, rejected by a total of 44 per cent, Chinese and Japanese, rejected by 33 per cent and finally the least unpopular group, the Southern European women, who are rejected by a mere 14 per cent.

In terms of *not* wanting men of other skin colours, the women in our survey reject *all* other groups quite firmly. The rejection of African and West Indian men and Indian and Pakistani men is almost the same, the least popular being the Indian and Pakistani men; rejected by 77 per cent, while the African and West Indian men are rejected by a total of 75 per cent. Men of Chinese or Japanese origin are rejected by 72 per cent, Middle Eastern men are rejected by a total of 69 per cent and finally South European men are rejected by a quite amazing total of 34 per cent of European women.

The two sets of statistics, for *both* men and women, can easily be seen in a sense as representing both sides of a coin. In terms of the exceedingly strong rejection of foreign men by the European women in our survey this surely has to do with the sort of outlook European women think these men have. It is probably accurate to say that they imagine such men are old-fashioned, excessively traditional, *macho*, especially given the situation overseas where they perceive the image of women in other cultures as *subservient*. They do not wish to swop places with such women. And by the same reasoning - as we have already argued - many European men perceive the situation in rather the same way, but place a very different value on it: for example, the fact that Chinese and Japanese women are the *least* rejected group by European men is probably largely due to both their exotic and subservient image.

If we turn to the **non-Europeans** in our survey - most of them want to meet Europeans, while Europeans are also the least rejected by them. Such Europeans are also *always* more desired than people of their *own* skin colour, racial type. Again such a fact is not especially surprising. For a start to be both successful and enjoy an easy passage through life in our western societies it helps to be one of the natives, so to speak. An Englishman in England tends to have an easier life than a Kenyan or indeed a 'West Indian' *born* in England. So the message is simple: if we cannot change the colour of our skin, at least we can marry someone of another skin. And of course as many European men, for example, see Thai women as 'exotic', many foreigners see Europeans similarly as being desirable - the case of Middle Eastern men and their infatuation with the 'English Rose' springs immediately to mind.

Specifically **Southern European** *men* want to meet European women (77 per cent) even more than their companion Southern European women (less than 59 per cent). Seventeen per cent are willing to accept Chinese or Japanese women, 14 per cent are willing to accept Middle Eastern women, 8 per cent Indian and Pakistani women, while only 3 per cent are willing to meet African and West Indian women. Southern European *women* wanting European men amount to a percentage of 74 as opposed to the 57 per cent who are willing to accept Southern European men. On the other hand only 7 per cent will accept Middle Eastern men, 4 per cent Chinese and Japanese men, 4 per cent African and West Indian men and a mere 2 per cent Indian and Pakistani men.

In terms of *rejection* only 1 per cent of Southern European *men reject* European women, while 2 per cent similarly reject Southern European women. Once again African and West Indian women are the least wanted - 62 per cent rejection, while 49 per cent reject Indian and Pakistani women, 31 per cent reject Chinese and Japanese women and 30 per cent reject Middle Eastern women. A similar pattern occurs with the rejection by South European *women* - only 1 per cent reject European men while 5 per cent reject South European men. The rejection of other groups is far stronger by the women - 74 per cent reject African and West Indian men, 73 per cent Indian and Pakistani men, 67 per cent reject Chinese and Japanese men, while finally 58 per cent reject Middle Eastern men.

If we turn to other groups, it is evident that although such groups indicate clearly that it is the Europeans they prefer, they nonetheless express high percentages of a willingness to consider people from other groups. So, for example, **African and West Indian** men clearly want to meet European women - indeed a total of 69 per cent, while the next most wanted group of people are African and West Indian women (42 per cent: this is indeed a high 'second choice' compared with the 'second choice' of other groups, but it should nonetheless be noted that there are still fewer than half of the African and West Indian men who want to meet African or West Indian women). The next most wanted group is of Southern European origin, 38 per cent, followed by Indian and Pakistani women, wanted by 22 per cent, then 20 per cent who are willing to meet Chinese and Japanese women, and also 20 per cent for Middle Eastern women.

The most popular men for African and West Indian women are, once more, European, with a total of 67 per cent, followed by African and West Indian men - 45 per cent (once again though this is less than half the total of African and West Indian women). Southern European men follow next - 34 per cent - then Middle Eastern - 11 per cent - and finally Chinese and Japanese men only wanted by 4 per cent.

In terms of absolute *rejection* only 3 per cent of African and West Indian *men* reject European women, while 8 per cent reject South European women, and 17 per cent reject their own African and West Indian women. The most rejected are Indian and Pakistani women - 28 per cent, followed by the

27 per cent rejection of Chinese and Japanese women, then finally Middle Eastern women rejected by 23 per cent.

Once again the two *least* rejected groups by African and West Indian *women* are European men (only 9 per cent reject them) and Southern European men (only 19 per cent reject them). The next *least rejected* group are their own African and West Indian men, with a total of 24 per cent not wishing to meet such individuals. If we dwell on this statistic for a moment, what it actually means is that almost a quarter of all African and West Indian women in the survey do not wish to meet their male counterparts. This can of course be viewed as a symptom of a multi-racial mentality or, more sadly, as a denial of one's roots, but more likely it is, as we have already argued, a reflection that life is easier if we are hitched to one who is an indigenous European.

The African and West Indian women in our survey most *reject* Indian and Pakistani men with a total of 60 per cent expressing such a feeling. The next most rejected group of people are the Chinese and Japanese men, rejected by 55 per cent and finally there are the men from the Middle East whom 41 per cent of African and West Indian women reject.

The **Chinese and Japanese** pattern is clear and extremely strong. Sixty-six per cent of Chinese and Japanese men want to meet European women, while 43 per cent of them want Chinese and Japanese women, a figure which actually only narrowly beats the 38 per cent who are willing to consider Southern European women. After these categories they are not that much interested - 10 per cent would consider Middle Eastern women, 4 per cent Indian and Pakistani women while 2 per cent would consider African and West Indian women. The pattern is also clear with the Chinese and Japanese *women*: 81 per cent want to meet European men but, unlike their male counterparts, Chinese and Japanese women pragmatically place Southern European men *before* Chinese and Japanese men with 26 per cent being prepared to accept Southern European men while only 20 per cent would accept Chinese and Japanese men. Finally 4 per cent would accept Middle Eastern men while less than 1 per cent would accept Indian and Pakistani men, a figure similar to those prepared to meet African and West Indian men.

If we look at *rejection*, very few Chinese and Japanese men reject Europeans (2 per cent) or Southern Europeans (7 per cent), but there are nearly a quarter, 22 per cent in fact, who are not interested in meeting Chinese and Japanese women. The most rejected group consists of African and West Indian women (75 per cent), while 62 per cent reject Indian and Pakistani women, while finally 46 per cent reject Middle Eastern women. Less than 1 per cent of Chinese and Japanese women do not want to meet European men, while only 15 per cent do not wish to meet Southern European men. However, nearly a third (33 per cent) do not want to meet Chinese and Japanese men. Finally the most rejected groups are African and West Indian men (77 per cent) followed by the Indians and Pakistanis (77 per cent), and Middle Eastern men (61 per cent).

Middle Eastern men do not break the pattern as 73 per cent of them want European women, while 46 per cent are willing to consider the Southern European women. The next most acceptable group is the Middle Eastern women, with 36 per cent of the men willing to consider them. Then come Indian and Pakistani women (18 per cent), Chinese and Japanese women (16 per cent) and finally only 5 per cent for African and West Indian women. Similar percentages are found among Middle Eastern women with 73 per cent of them willing to consider European men and 46 per cent of them willing to consider Southern European men.

There is a higher percentage of Middle Eastern women willing to consider Middle Eastern men than *vice versa*, but given both the certainty and force of the Islamic faith this perhaps is not too surprising. Indeed perhaps the fact that they are willing to consider so many of the *other groups* is the most surprising observation to make.

Following their willingness to meet European, Southern European and Middle Eastern men, 10 per cent of the survey's Middle Eastern women are prepared to meet Chinese and Japanese men, followed by the 6 per cent prepared to meet Indian or Pakistani men, with finally 5 per cent willing to meet African and West Indian men.

Very few Middle Eastern men *reject* the idea of meeting European or Southern European women, indeed less than 1 per cent expresses any such rejection. Thirteen per cent of such men do *not* wish to meet Middle Eastern women, while 60 per cent do not wish to meet African and West Indian women, and 36 per cent reject the idea of meeting Indian and Pakistani women. Chinese and Japanese women are rejected by about 28 per cent of men from the Middle East.

Once again with the case of Middle Eastern women very few indeed, less than 3 per cent in fact, *reject* European men, and only 11 per cent reject Southern European men. Almost 20 per cent, however, reject Middle Eastern men while African and West Indian men are most rejected, by a total of 69 per cent. Fifty-eight per cent reject Indian and Pakistani men, while the Chinese and Japanese men are rejected by 53 per cent.

Finally we turn to the **Indian and Pakistani group**, where over 60 per cent of the men want to meet European women with 43 per cent wishing to meet those from Southern Europe. They are also willing to meet women from their own groups - over 47 per cent are willing to meet Indian and Pakistani women. This of course is the legacy of the tradition of arranged marriages, where relationships were steered firmly into the familiar territory of same caste, same religion, same region. Twenty-six per cent of these men are willing to meet Middle Eastern women and 26 per cent of them are willing to meet Chinese and Japanese women. Only 6 per cent want African and West Indian women.

In terms of the top three categories the women follow the pattern of the men. Sixty-three per cent wish to meet European men while 31 per cent want to meet Southern European men. They are not quite as interested as the men in meeting people of their own group but nonetheless the figure is still quite high, being 37 per cent. The next most popular group is Middle Eastern men, 12 per cent being willing to meet them. Only 6 per cent are willing to meet Chinese and Japanese men, and 3 per cent are interested in meeting African and West Indian men.

Very few Indian and Pakistani men *reject* European women, indeed only 2 per cent, with 5 per cent rejecting Southern European women. Thirteen per cent do not wish to meet women from their own group while the most unpopular group are African and West Indian women with 57 per cent not wishing to meet them. Twenty-two per cent do not want to meet Chinese and Japanese women, while 17 per cent do not want to meet Middle Eastern women.

There is more of a rejection of European and Southern European men among the Indian and Pakistani women with 8 per cent not wishing to meet European men and 17 per cent not wanting Southern European men. On the other hand they have a higher percentage of rejecting men from their own group with 30 per cent not wanting to meet Indian and Pakistani men. The least popular are African and West Indian men, with almost 80 per cent of the Asian women not wishing to meet them. Almost 60 per cent have no desire to meet Chinese and Japanese men, while Middle Eastern men are rejected by approximately 46 per cent of Asian women.

In the chapter which follows we briefly *summarize* what we have so far discovered from our foray into both the self-descriptions of those taking part in our survey, together with what they have said they require, or desire in their partners in terms of basic characteristics.

Chapter Two:

So what do we really want?

> He is a chump, you know. That's
> what I love about him. That and the
> way his ears wiggle when he gets
> excited. Chumps always make the
> best husbands. When you marry,
> Sally, grab a chump. Tap his fore-
> head first, and if it rings solid, don't
> hesitate. All the unhappy marriages
> come from the husband having
> brains. What good are brains to a
> man? They only unsettle him.
>
> P.G. WODEHOUSE

A brief perusal of the results of our survey suggest a
slightly different picture to the one painted by
Wodehouse. Certainly it seems that the *men*, rather
than the women, are less concerned with their
partner's brain power - physical attributes appear
more important to them.

In the previous chapter our survey of 'ordinary
people' in search of a partner told us what they were
looking and not looking for. This should give us a
rough idea of what they might well end up getting, for
better or for worse. Such individuals may well be
searching for someone who is quite wrong for them.
They could be basing their 'ideal partner' on incorrect
assumptions, on stereotyped ideas on who is desirable
and who is not. Choices could be based on

misunderstanding, misinformation. And of course our deep psyches have a part in all of this: we may be choosing partners because of some hidden urge or sentiment or memory, quite unbeknown to us. Like the proverbial iceberg, the processes leading to our choosing may well be powerfully out of view.

So, we begin our quest for our ideal perfect partner. For better or for worse - for who amongst us knows precisely how *our* particular relationship will work out over time - we are determined to find the kind of person we believe is ideally suited to us.

What we must understand from the outset is that we are not implying that the meeting of a partner is pre-planned and that therefore such things as 'love at first sight' do not exist. However, once we have it in our head that we know the kind of person who will make us 'happy' in a relationship, it is likely that we will exclude from our daily and social life those people who do not measure up to our ideal. In other words, a successful, non-smoking, non-drinking, devout church-goer with an eye for beauty and a wish for a similar mate, is unlikely to put themselves in a position to meet a smoking, drinking, overweight, unemployed atheist, even though that person could be just the one to make them happy. Because we have in our mind a definite set of qualities for our 'ideal partner', we are not going to make an opportunity to meet a person who is just the opposite, even though 'love at first sight' might well take place if we did.

We rule out of consideration all sorts of people, by virtue of their age, height, build, nationality, skin, religion, politics; without even getting close enough to examine their personalities. And of course we know that we could face a lengthy - and perhaps unfruitful - struggle to convince those who we believe would make ideal partners for us, that we ourselves would make ideal partners for them!

Moreover the escalating divorce rate might well be a reflection of a number of factors:

- we never did meet the person we knew would have been **ideal** for us, either because we never **found** them or that we did in fact do so but they turned us down;
- or, that we believed we had indeed found our ideal partner, but that it turned out not to be true;
- or, that we never did meet our ideal person so therefore we had to cope with second best with the inevitable result of failure.

More likely, other things were at work:

- we indeed *did* meet our 'ideal' partner but that over time it became apparent that they were not so 'ideal' after all;
- because we had misunderstood our *real* needs, or that our choice of 'ideal partner' had in the first place been based on spurious assumptions;
- or, because, quite simply, one or both of us had changed *over time*, so what was 'ideal' when we met, was not in fact the case some years and years later.

We are merely hinting at the complexity of the matter in hand. Indeed it really is a tragic irony that we genuinely do not put much thought into what happens to relationships *over time*, while so much effort goes into meeting someone in the first place. Especially as so much of our initial thoughts on what is the perfect partner consists of fantasies, rather than realities; let alone the absolute certainty that none of us stay the same over time.

It is most likely that we will *never* end up with exactly what we thought we were looking for in the first place, even if we *truly* knew what we wanted.

The hurdles preventing us from finding happiness in relationships are, therefore, numerous and varied. We may have it all wrong; our motivations and ideas as to the perfect partner could be misplaced; there may not be enough tall, slender, white, European, liberal, Roman Catholic individuals around who, also, needless to say, enjoy the Rolling Stones *and* Mozart, are kind and considerate *and*, nonetheless, forceful. And so on.

Take the even more basic fact of numbers. Are there enough of each of us to go round in the first place? Quite a question. An analysis of our own survey in terms of age, sex and marital status is, in itself, quite revealing.

To begin with there are certainly more single people in the survey than any other category, and the greatest number of them fall in the age range 21 to 39 years. The percentage of single women in the 16 to 20 category is far greater than that of men - only 6 per cent of all single men are to be found there whereas 17 per cent of single women are in that category. In the survey there are far more single men between 21 and 29 than women - 6905 men compared with 2146 women - but in terms of the percentage of total single men and the percentage of total single women, 54 per cent of single men fall into this category while 42 per cent of single women are between 21 and 29.

When we get to the 30 to 39 years age range there are again many more men than women - 4030 men compared with 1573 women - but the percentage totals of this group compared with all single men/women is similar: 32 per cent of all single men are in this category, and 31 per cent of all single women. Again at the age band 40 to 59 years, there are more men than women, though what they represent as a percentage of the totals is similar - 8 per cent of all single men are in the category and 9 per cent of single women.

Looking at the later years, at 60 plus, there are more single men than women, although they represent similar percentages of the totals of each sex.

The greatest numbers of widows and widowers are found between the years of 40 and 59. Sixty-one per cent of widows and 74 per cent of widowers are found there. The rather interesting figure with regard to widows and widowers is in the 30 to 39 years category where there are many more widows than widowers, representing 8 per cent of all widowers and 10 per cent of all widows. At the top of the age range there is a much more significant difference - many more widows than widowers over the age of 60. In terms of percentages there is also a great deal of difference, with the numbers representing 30 per cent of all widowers but only 15 per cent of widows.

This set of statistics appertaining to the widowed reflects national trends. Put bluntly, as women generally tend to outlive men, male spouses depart this earth earlier than their partners - especially as they usually start off in such partnerships being older than their companions. Similarly the earlier statistic of there being far more single men than single women in the age range of 20 to 29 years, both reflects national trends and also points to the problems engaged in meeting our dream partners.

Specifically: if a male desires to meet a single young woman of a similar age to himself he clearly has a lot of competition! And this is *before* the processes and nuances of attraction, or indeed the possibilities of a relationship developing are even started.

Finally in terms of marriages which have come to an end, by far the largest numbers are in the *divorced* category. For example there are in the 30 to 39 age range, 1489 divorced men compared with 593 separated men in the same age range. The same occurs with women - 1266 divorced women compared with 358 separated women. The greatest numbers of divorced people, not surprisingly, are to be found in the 40 to 59 category where there are 2035 men and 2456 women. These figures represent 52 per cent of all divorced men and 61 per cent of all divorced women. Interestingly enough here we see a category in which there are *more women than men*.

Again these statistics demonstrate the reliability of our survey as a reflection of national trends, and, more importantly, demonstrate how perhaps our ideal choices of partners are forced into compromise. By virtue, for example, of the ever-increasing numbers of divorced women to be found within the 40 to 59 years range - and in greater numbers than divorced men - taken in tandem with the greater numbers of single *younger* men, we see the origins of the newer patterns of relationships between younger men and older women. *Toy boys*, to you and me. This is not to say that such older divorced women would necessarily ideally wish to meet older men, it is just simply to point to some of the basic hurdles we have to overcome in our search for our 'ideal' partner.

Battle of the sexes?

Much of what goes on within the private walls of a relationship often resembles a battlefield - our own bruises and feelings of hurt testify to the fact, let alone the more public evidence seen in the divorce courts and the casualty wards. Often it seems, simply but painfully so, that men and women actually want different things from each other, desire different things, and value different aspects of their relationships. Certainly many couples have to fight the *gender war* before they fight their own little personal wars, or indeed perhaps each war is waged side by side.

Not only are marriages and other intimate relationships prone to trouble and strife, and not only do such relationships at times exemplify the differences between men and women, but additionally they are full of mystery. How many times have we heard the plaintive cries of: 'What does she see in him?'; 'I don't know why he puts up with it'; 'He's so much better looking than her'; 'They argue and fight all the time, but they're still together'; 'She's so young, and not very bright, and he's so clever - what do they see in each other?', and other such everyday observations. As a matter of fact, it is this very mystery that often holds the key to why some people are attracted to each other and stay together, despite their appearing an unlikely pairing. And it is something we quite clearly cannot define. Such mysteries remain mysteries.

What we can do here, however, is to point to those very differences (and indeed similarities) between men and women as they list the priorities they seek in their potential perfect partners. We can, generally speaking, recognize what men and women are looking for in potential companions and lovers, an attitude which will both guide their search and colour any relationships they may well eventually enter into. And as we have earlier argued, an individual man or woman's attitude in these matters rules out all number of (quite possibly ideal) potential partners, without even exchanging a polite 'hello'.

To begin with it has to be accepted that we are not - not all of us, at least - utterly unrealistic or stupid. Most of us *do* realize that we can't have anything or anybody. Many of us may well drool over all sorts of role models - Gracie Fields, David Niven, Elizabeth Taylor, Michael Caine, Paul McCartney, Elvis, Warren Beatty, Robert Redford, Madonna, Maradona - but know intuitively that we ourselves will never attract anyone quite like them, neither are we ourselves very special. Instead we settle for what we see as far more realistic - most of us define ourselves as 'averagely attractive'. Indeed any self-respecting psychologist will say we tend to choose people quite like ourselves. However, let us be more specific and recall what was expressed in our survey.

Marital Status

Despite general agreement between the sexes, slightly more women than men are turned off by the previously unmarried - single men. Men are far less keen to need women who have lived through earlier marriages and divorce. We are, however, only talking about the majority; there are members of both sexes who are prepared to meet divorced individuals. The separated are less wanted. Women are more prepared than men to embrace the widowed.

Physical attributes.

Not surprisingly people see themselves as 'average', in terms of 'attractiveness'. Men are extremely keen to meet 'slim' women, and similarly women desire 'slim' men, if a little less so.

Habits.

If you are a single smoker, begin reading a lengthy novel or take up meditation, for smokers are not especially welcomed by either sex. Drinkers are more acceptable - especially if they are 'occasional drinkers' - and more specifically, male drinking is a little more acceptable than female drinking.

Religion, education and politics.

Women appear to feel more strongly about matters spiritual than men do, and, in the survey, certainly feel negative towards atheists. Islam is not popular with either sex. A major difference occurs in the sphere of education: quite simpl women are more interested in meeting educationally qualified men than vice versa.

Politics on the other hand neither excites too many individuals, nor does it greatly divide the sexes in terms of opinion. People of the 'centre' are valued, while those of the 'right' and 'left' are not so popular. Women are slightly more definite than men about politics.

Racial types, racial stereotypes

The matter is detailed - witness the earlier exhaustive survey - yet in essence, it is also quite simple. Generally speaking both European *and* non-European male and females wish, predominantly, to meet Europeans. There is very little evidence of either high-risk, inter-racial mixing or of non-European individuals determined to continue and develop their heritage.

Conclusion

So how may we conclude? Well the picture that emerges is that the majority of both sexes are basically in agreement over the majority of dimensions, with a few disagreements.

Men generally *prefer* attractive, slim, educationally average, non-smoking, occasionally drinking, marginally religious, politically centred, European, single women, of smaller height to themselves and a few years younger. Women generally *prefer* attractive, slim, well-educated, non-smoking, occasionally drinking, religious, politcally centred, European men who need not necessarily be single (they could well be divorced), of taller height than themselves and similarly possibly older than they are themselves.

As we saw earlier, in some particular age groups there are simply not enough people - live bodies! - to go round. Ask any widow of 60, or a youth of 19 - especially if he lives in a small isolated village. Moreover not all of us can refrain from smoking, eating too much or consistently voting for left-wing political parties. Similarly none of us is to blame if we possess all the desired qualities - don't smoke, drink only in moderation, etc. - yet are less than 5 feet tall.

Somehow most of us find somebody to love - and maybe subsequently, and, sadly, not infrequently to hate; or perhaps live an unfulfilled life with. We have seen what are the *basic* factors individual men and women look for in their search for love, partners and companionship. Now - by looking at those couples who *have* met and are (currently) in seemingly successful relationships - we must learn more about the less tangible aspects of such arrangements. We must seek answers to such questions as:

- **How important is sex within our relationships?**
- **Do men communicate enough with their partners?**
- **Can friends help us cope with our marital crises?, and many others.**

PART TWO: COUPLEDOM

Chapter Three:
The State of the Art

I have seen the failure of too many
marriages, and warmed my hands
before a few glowing successes, and
in every case have thought and
examined and wondered, and never
found any logic, for marriage is as
mysterious as life or fire. I know
only that there is no objective existence to it. It cannot be studied from
the outside and conclusions drawn,
for it lives only inside itself, and
what is presented to the observer or
the listener bears only the relationship of a distorted shadow to the
reality inside.

JOHN MASTERS

Like the above perceptive writer, we all have seen
both successful *and* less-fruitful marriages,
relationships and companionships. Some of us have
been in such relationships ourselves. Indeed many of
us still bear the scars, while the lucky ones amongst
us may still be wallowing in the joy good
relationships inevitably bring. Whichever way it may
have turned out for ourselves, we all - regardless of
our histories - relentlessly pursue our dream partners.
All of us follow the path we hope will lead to love and
happiness. It is hardly surprising, of course, that we

pursue such a possibility, for from childhood onwards we are all steered to marriage relationships, of one kind or another.

If marriage falls apart, we eventually seem to do it all over again. Re marriage is less the taboo subject that it once was not so very long ago. The thrice-divorced actress Shelley Winters amusingly comments that she had eventually 'discovered that I like getting married but I don't like *being* married,' and adds that 'it would have helped if I'd realized that before my trips to the altar.'

Indeed in the same way that we all wish to make children yet know so little about parenthood, similarly we all want to be married (or its equivalent) yet know almost nothing about what it will bring: how it will test us, how we will have to learn how to share and compromise, how we will have no alternative but to experience both the pleasure *and* pain of intimacy, how sex can be used as a weapon, how the arrival of children can alter dramatically the dynamics of a relationship, and so on. What currently is the state of the art - of marriage *and* divorce?

It helps to start with statistics - figures which will help confirm an individual's experience, and also provide a context for the often varied matrimonial lives people lead.

A Changing World

It is not simply our marital lives which have changed over the decades. Many features of our social and individual lives have altered.

For example:

- **The two million people aged over 80 years of age now living in Britain is 50 per cent greater than in 1961.**

- In 1971 *women* formed 37 per cent of the British labour force; shortly it will have risen to over 44 per cent.

- Between 1971 and 1988 the proportion of 'illegitimate' births in Britain increased from one in twelve births to one in four. (Interestingly enough although illegitimacy in Britain in 1987 was higher than in West Germany, the Netherlands, Italy, Australia and Canada, it was lower than in France, Sweden, Denmark and the USA).

- While lone parents with young children formed less than 5 per cent of all households in 1987, nonetheless 14 per cent of children lived their lives with only one parent - double the figure of 1971.

- Significantly, one of the most notable features of post-World War II has been the increase in people living alone: in 1988 over a quarter of households in Britain contained only one person, compared with about one-eighth in 1961.

Before we examine more closely the bare facts of the changing face of *marriage and divorce*, let us experience a few more statistics:

- Married couples remain the backbone of British domestic life. For example in 1987 married couples with dependent children formed 44 per cent of all households, while married couples with adult children or no children at all comprised one third of all households.

- The UK also heads the EC's *divorce* league, an honour it shares with Denmark.

- However, the UK is also equal top with Portugal for the EC *marriage* rate.

70

■ In England and Wales in 1988, seven out of every ten divorce decrees were granted to *wives*, and in more than half of these the main reason cited for the 'irretrievable breakdown' of the marriage was the husband's unreasonable behaviour. His adultery was cited in just under 30 per cent of cases.

Marriage and divorce: EC comparison, 1981 and 1987

	Rate			
	Marriages per 1000 eligible population		Divorces per 1000 marriages	
	1981	1987	1981	1987
United Kingdom	7.1	7.0	11.9	12.6
Belgium	6.5	5.7	6.1	7.8
Denmark	5.0	6.1	12.1	12.7
France	5.8	4.7	6.8	8.5*
Germany (Fed. Rep.)	5.8	6.3	7.2	8.8
Greece	7.3	6.6	2.5	3.0†
Irish Republic	6.0	5.1	0.0	0.0
Italy	5.6	5.3	0.9	1.8
Luxembourg	5.5	5.3	5.9	7.5†
Netherlands	6.0	6.0	8.3	8.1
Portugal	7.7	7.0	2.8	
Spain	5.4	5.3*	1.1	

*1986   † 1985
Source: Statistical Office of the European Communities

The Marriage-go-round

We are sometimes in danger of not paying enough attention to the quite staggering changes taking place. Examine closely the table below:

Marriages: by type United Kingdom					
	1961	1971	1976	1987	1988
Marriages (thousands)					
First marriage for both partners	340	369	282	260	253
First marriage for one partner only					
Bachelor/divorced woman	11	21	30	34	34
Bachelor/widow	5	4	4	2	2
Spinster/divorced man	12	24	32	39	39
Spinster/widower	8	5	4	2	2
Second (or subsequent) marriage for both partners					
Both divorced	5	17	34	47	50
Both widowed	10	10	10	5	5
Divorced man/widow	3	4	5	4	4
Divorced woman/widower	3	5	5	5	5
Total marriages	397	459	406	398	394
Remarriages* as a percentage of all marriages	14	20	31	35	36
Remarriages of the divorced as a percentage of all marriages	9	15	26	32	33

* Remarriages for one or both partners
Source: Office of Population Censuses and Surveys

■ **In 1988, in one third of all British marriages one party was a divorcee. Marriages between bachelors and spinsters accounted for 64 per cent of marriages, compared with 86 per cent at the beginning of the 1960s.**

In England and Wales in 1988, seven out of every ten divorce decrees were granted to *wives*, and in more than half of these the main reason cited for the 'irretrievable breakdown' of the marriage was the husband's unreasonable behaviour. His adultery was cited in just under 30 per cent of cases.

Take, for example, the rate in the above table for second marriages in which both partners are divorced. In 1961 only 5000 such marriages were recorded, whereas now the figures have risen to 50000. Notwithstanding the fact that legal changes (notably the *Divorce Reform Act 1969*) have made it easier to divorce, the rate of the remarriages of the divorced as a percentage of all marriages has risen from 9 per cent in 1961 to a current staggering 33 per cent.

Another interesting statistic refers to racial types: white European men are most likely to be married (52 per cent) as are Indian women (52 per cent) while West Indian and African men and women are the most likely to be divorced (4 per cent and 6 per cent respectively) or separated. Almost 12 per cent of white European women are widowed, a far higher percentage than any of the ethnic minority populations.

So the people in our survey reluctant to meet West Indian and African individuals *may* have been influenced by the fact that their divorce and separation rate is the highest.

The number of marriages each year depends partly on the age and marital status structure of the population and, of course, on the ratio of males to females. Changes in the number of marriages could therefore reflect the changing size and characteristics of the population eligible to marry. Marriage, remarriage and divorce rates for men and women are shown below in terms of numbers per thousand eligible. The remarriage rate for men increased substantially during the 1960s and early 1970s reaching a peak in 1972s, the year after the *Divorce Reform Act 1969* came into force in England and Wales. Since 1972 the rate of remarriages for men has fallen in most years, and in 1988 the rate was two thirds that of the 1972 peak, at a level comparable with that recorded in the mid-sixties. For women, the changes in the remarriage rate over time have been much more gradual: the rate rose sharply in 1972, and since then has remained fairly stable. In 1988 the remarriage rate per eligible man was two and a half times the corresponding rate for women, though the actual number of remarriages is similar. The rates of first marriages, have fallen since 1972.

Considering all that we have said earlier, it is of no surprise that the remarriage rate of women has been both more stable and lower than that of men. Men clearly need to marry in order to give themselves an identity they are happy with; women can define themselves more easily without their marital status, and may well have learned more from one marriage and its pitfalls than men have; women are usually left to care for the children following divorce, and therefore it may well be more difficult for the divorced woman to marry, as compared with the footloose and fancy-free divorced male.

Marriage, remarriage and divorce: by sex Great Britain

1 Irrespective of partner's marital status

2 The Divorce Reform Act 1969 came into effect in England and Wales on 1 January 1971

Marriage, remarriage and divorce: by sex
Great Britain

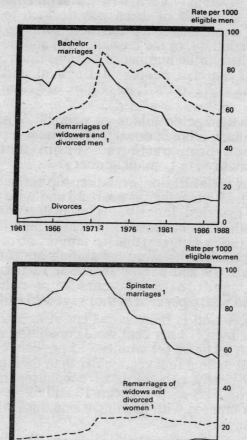

Rate per 1000 eligible men

Bachelor marriages [1]

Remarriages of widowers and divorced men [1]

Divorces

1961   1966   1971 [2]   1976   1981   1986   1988

Rate per 1000 eligible women

Spinster marriages [1]

Remarriages of widows and divorced women [1]

Divorces

1961   1966   1971 [2]   1976   1981   1986   1988

1. Irrespective of partner's marital status
2. The Divorce Reform Act 1969 came into effect in England and Wales on 1 January 1971

   Source: Office of Population Censuses and Surveys

We have already noted that of divorce decrees granted in England and Wales in 1988, seven out of ten were given to women, *wives*, and that the 'cause' of more than half of these was deemed to be the husband's unreasonable behaviour; followed then by cases of adultery, of the husband. An additional fact is that whereas the number of *persons divorcing per thousand married people* in England and Wales amounted to 2.1 in 1961, this figure had risen to 12.8 in 1988.

At what stage do things go wrong? When does communication break down? When does a partner - or indeed both partners - begin to behave 'unreasonably', or commit adultery?

Finally **cohabitation**, a relationship defined as two persons living together as husband and wife without having married legally. The prevalence for cohabitation has increased in Great Britain in recent years; estimates suggest that the proportion of women aged 18 to 49 who were cohabiting almost tripled between 1979 and 1988. In 1988, 12 per cent of women aged 18 to 24 years were cohabiting compared with 6 per cent of those aged 25 to 49 years.

Cohabitation is more prevalent at ages 25 to 29 years for men (13 per cent were cohabiting in 1988) and 20 to 24 years for women (15 per cent cohabit); men tend to be a few years older than their partners. In 1988 nearly two thirds of cohabiting men and women in 1988 aged between 16 and 59 years were single compared with just under one third who were divorced.

So what on earth makes people continue to marry, to hope, to search for love, to seek companionship? In the next chapter we put flesh on the bare bones, listening to detailed accounts of another group of individuals - *couples* who believe they have indeed at last found love, companionship and happiness.

Divorce: by duration of marriage

	Percentages and thousands Year of divorce									
Duration of marriage (completed years)										
0-2	1.2	1.2	1.5	1.5	1.3	1.2	8.9	9.2	9.3	9.5
3-4	10.1	12.2	16.5	19.0	19.5	19.6	18.8	15.3	13.7	13.4
5-9	30.6	30.5	30.2	29.1	28.7	28.3	26.2	27.5	28.6	28.0
10-14	22.9	19.4	18.7	19.6	19.2	18.9	17.1	17.5	17.5	17.5
15-19	13.9	12.6	12.8	12.8	12.9	13.2	12.2	12.8	13.0	13.2
20-24		9.5	8.8	8.6	8.6	8.7	7.9	8.4	8.7	9.1
25-29	21.2	5.8	5.6	4.9	5.2	5.3	4.7	4.8	4.9	4.9
30 & over	58.9	5.9	4.5	4.7	4.6	4.2	4.3	4.3	4.3	
All durations (= 100%)										
(thousands)	27.0	79.2	135.4	155.6	160.7	156.4	173.7	166.7	163.1	

Source: Office of Population Censuses and Surveys

As can be seen from the above table, the problematic period for any marriage is especially after five years of marriage and prior to the conclusion of a decade. The rate of 30 per cent of divorces within this period of completed time has remained pretty stable over the years. Once more, although legal changes have affected a number of the rates, the evidence that on the one hand almost 10 per cent of divorces follow on from less than two years of a completed marriage, while on the other 4 per cent of divorces follow on from over 30 years of marriage, does suggest that marriage is a pretty unstable state of affairs to be involved in. If you can excuse the pun.

Chapter Four:
LOVE IS ...

It is true that I never should have married, but I didn't want to live without a man. Brought up to respect the conventions, love had to end in marriage. I'm afraid it did.

BETTE DAVIS

We are not conceding defeat when we say that in this chapter we cannot offer the reader the comfort of statistics. Although statistics allow us some certainty to our judgements, allow us to make some comparisons and measure changes over time, we also have to be realistic and acknowledge that not everything *can* be measured, weighed up or compared.This is the position that we are placed in now; in this chapter we are concerned with the feelings and opinions the members of our survey hold with respect to such intangible matters as definitions of love, feelings about intimacy and sexuality, the *precise* effect that the arrival of children have on a relationship, who should do which tasks in the home, and other such matters of our love lives. Inevitably various individuals will hold varied views, or express similar views but with varying degrees of strength. Not all of us agree as to what matters most in the realm of our personal, intimate lives.

Indeed it is abundantly clear that disagreements as to what truly is important within relationships are at the basis of the dissolution of marital and other partnerships. And the likelihood of the success of communication to resolve the issue is remote. Indeed it is increasingly clear that a major, significant difference between the sexes is that very fact of communication: we regularly hear one partner (usually, but not necessarily, the female) complain that their partner 'no longer talks to them.

So what *can* we discover about such issues? In a nutshell our survey may well confirm some of the more basic, statistical points we have earlier made and also it will allow us to spell out both the variety and strength of individual feelings and thoughts. Finally, and most importantly, the result of the survey will allow us to make some reasonably well-researched guesses - measured intuitions if you like - as to the nature of the love search.

What follows then are some further results of our survey, more specifically an investigation into the beliefs and feelings of couples who believe they *have* at last found love and who presently are ensconsed within such relationships.

Definitions of Love.

We spend so much of our time both talking about love and believing we are 'in love', yet spend little time fathoming out what it actually means. We respond with certainty, however, if we're asked the question 'Are you in love?' And we confidently claim we know when love has gone from our lives. But what is it? What does the condition consist of? Is it, quite simply, something beyond words, without description, something only possible to experience? A 22-year-old previously single civil servant, considers that:

'Being in love means *trust* and *companionship*, *sharing* the good and bad times and knowing that it is all worth it,'

and in response to the question 'do you think there are definite phases in love - for example do you think that there is an early exciting/idyllic phase which will almost certainly wear off in time?', she agreed:

'Yes I think so, but I feel that it *settles down* and is much nicer, you don't have to put on an act.'

Her partner, a 24-year-old decorator, was certain that he was 'in love':

'I *feel inside* that I'm in love, I look at her in the morning and I feel warm towards her. I want to be with her. I constantly think about her ... I define love as knowing the other person makes you feel *wanted* and *needed*.'

He considered that the 'bad things' about being in love consisted, essentially, of being 'taken for granted'.

Another couple, again both previously single, a little older, both being 31 years old, expressed similar thoughts and feelings:

Female: 'I can't wait for him to come home ... love is, a *deep and intense feeling* of *affection* and trust and of wanting to *share one's life* with someone and giving your all to make that person happy.'

Male: 'Love is ... the *sharing of enjoyment, sadness* and all emotions ... and, is a knowing in your heart.'

They were in no doubt as to the power of what they saw to be love, and when she first realized she was in love, was euphoric: 'I couldn't eat or sleep or concentrate. It started to affect my work.' Both felt such a strong sense was symptomatic of the fact that love had its stages, its phases. She, as she indicated, couldn't eat or sleep in the beginning, then she felt more 'comfortable', with feelings of '*contentment*' . Her partner agreed there was an initial idyllic phase, but also felt that love did develop yet remained 'fresh.'

A couple, both in their fifties, both previously divorced, expressed *their* feelings as follows:

Female: 'Love is *caring for someone who cares for you*, it adds to a totally different meaning to living, and a brighter outlook on life.'

Male: 'Love is a feeling of *contentment, security*, and well-being and confidence in your partner.'

Both felt that love gave them a *purpose in life* , with the essential factor of companionship, although he also mentioned the negative, or potentially negative side to love, namely the ability to be hurt by one's partner, the feeling of vulnerability.

Another couple, again both previously divorced, with a 10-year age gap between them - he being 47 years old, and a manager - show no signs of any lingering bitterness about their pasts, and positively stress the joys of a loving relationship:

Female: 'I am excited before we meet after a day's work. I want to surprise him (meals, presents, dresses I wear).'

Male: 'Love is ... a complete encompassing aura of *happiness, contentment, fulfillment*, and wishing the same for your partner.'

For this couple, especially for her, 'being in love' was the most central aspect of life: 'life is exciting, suspense is in the air ... but there is also uncertainty, *he may not love me tomorrow* , where is he tonight ?... when you phone and no one answers.'

Ironically enough it is an older couple, a 69-year-old widower and his 55-year-old ex-divorcee, who first mention the element of sex in their definition of love:

81

Female: '*To love and be loved* makes the rest of life fall into *perspective* and all the ups and downs bearable.'

Male: 'Love is ... a *sexual need* with close *intimate* contact, plus *missing* her when not together.'

Neither of them felt that there was anything wrong with being in love, no lurking dangers and, despite having previously been divorced, she felt that love gave her 'a warmth, *a sense of security*', and that it was a '*very deep rooted need of all humans*.'

Of course their particular marital combination-an ex widower, an ex-divorcee - allowed them potentially extra insights into the stages which love might well travel through. Indeed, interestingly, she made the point that there were certainly stages involved yet believed that the state of love could remain the same 'if both *work* at it.'

Although there were a few minority views expressed, the previous definitions of love represent the average views of the survey. Throughout, a similar set of terms were expressed.

Many of the descriptive terms used in the definitions suggest that their partner had given them what they needed in order to cease their search. Many of the couples talk of 'settling down', of security, contentment, fulfilment, of feeling 'comfortable', of being wanted, of feeling warm inside, of being needed, of happiness and of affection. In a sense it is as if the individuals concerned were incomplete people until they met their partners who subsequently made them whole persons.

Certainly the most commonly used terms related to the notion of companionship and with it the related condition of sharing: the *sharing* of both joy and sadness, the sharing of enjoyment as well as of crises. By definition sharing, like companionship, is a two-way thing and this two-way aspect to these relationships - often emerged in the definitions, with much talk of 'caring for someone who cares for you', and of 'loving and being loved.'

Such an emphasis necessarily leads to a belief in the importance of *trust*, a quality much discussed by the survey. There was certainly a strength of feeling about the power and strength of love, with many individuals talking of being hurt, of missing partners, of not being 'loved tomorrow', but although many people clearly fear one of the other possibilities of love - abandonment - a more frequently expressed *direct* complaint is that of being 'taken for granted.'

Although most individuals recognized that love *did* go through stages and that, in a sense, the excitement would wear off, none were prepared merely to sit back and be taken for granted. This was partly due, of course, to the fact that for most people love and what it usually leads to - companionship, marriage - is *the* most important event in life. As one person put it, love puts everything into perspective, it offers a purpose to life; indeed, someone declared that they believed love to be a 'very deep rooted need of all humans.'

Intimacy and companionship were stressed far more than sexuality. Although all of our couples led active sexual lives, very few mentioned sex in their definitions of love. If there is a slight difference between the genders it is, not surprisingly perhaps, *men* who actually raise the issue. But even those men are in a considerably small minority. Most individuals appear to recognize - perhaps partly in hindsight, given the number of divorcees in our survey - that 'love' (at least the word!) signifies something different from purely sexual relations.

For the majority of our couples there was a disinterest in sexual relations with a partner of the *same sex* . Most people expressed the view that there was nothing intrinsically wrong with 'gay behaviour' but that it was 'not for them'. Some individuals felt that such behaviour was 'perfectly normal', while a small minority believed such people should be punished - 'strung up', as one person put it.

Surprisingly enough very few couples seemed particularly concerned about issues of birth control. All sorts of techniques and devices were mentioned: recurrent comments included those that the 'pill helped control painful periods', that the 'sheath could break', that 'he's had a vasectomy' and so on. Quite a number of couples complained that condoms made 'love making less romantic'. The majority of couples realized that decisions about birth control ought to be joint ones. Sadly, not all were aware of this, as is evident from this thirty-year-old couple:

Female: 'Yes, the pill. It is easy to take and reliable.'

Male: 'My partner is in charge of birth control. The advantages are not getting pregnant or not smelling of burning rubber - there are no disadvantages with the pill.'

'Being in love', and loving someone

For about half of the individuals concerned, their subsequent relationships developed out of situations of 'love at first sight'. People were extremely certain about this: it *either* definitely felt like love at first sight, or it didn't. Moreover there was little difference between those who felt love at first sight and those who didn't, in respect of gender, age or previous marital status. It is extremely difficult to say anything definite, constructive or significant about the situation. Many individuals clearly see another individual, are physically attracted by their appearance and possibly some minimal aspect of their personalities and proceed to develop their sense of attraction; or, as they tend to put it, to immediately fall in love, and continue to do so.

Perhaps three extremely tentative comments can be made about the matter. First, *as a strategy*, falling in love at first sight is not to be considered in too positive a light. We cannot know much about the person we immediately fall in love with - merely the colour of their hair, their eyes, their laugh, their body shape, and so on. And once hooked, it may only be a matter of time before we discover less agreeable sides to them, but by then it could be too late. Second, love (and marriage) takes place over time, in stages perhaps, and what were attractive aspects of our partner on first meeting may not be quite so agreeable in the later years. It *would* appear to make more sense if we got to know the *depth* of our partner's personality, the *range* of their interests, abilities and desires. However that leads to our third observation: 'love at first sight', like luck, might well be one of those elements which in total *do* constitute the mysterious aspect of successful (and not so successful) relationships.

For some people 'love at first sight' may well be the shorthand for that very idyllic, exciting, short-lived period at the beginning of relationships that many in our survey recognized. Certainly we do appear to recognize the difference between 'being in love' and loving someone:

Female: 'You can be in love with someone without them knowing it. Loving someone means you express your love.'

Male: 'Being in love is the start of a one to one relationship. Loving someone is similar, but more in the context of family love .'

Another couple reiterated this last theme:

Female: 'Loving your children is a more protecting love, whereas loving your husband is more selfish.'

Male: 'Being in love is more passionate than loving your children, for instance.'

One 37-year-old teacher expressed the general sentiment, when she argued that **'being in love will fade, loving will keep on and on going. But,'** she added cautiously, **'one can and must repeatedly give each other chances to fall in love again ... it can be done.'** Another generally well-held view was that while we could be in love with someone without caring, 'loving involves *caring* deeply.'

So once more there is an emphasis on the more *tender*, if you like, aspects to these relationships rather than the more excitingly-coloured emotions. It is certainly evident that if we are to survive or enjoy long-term relationships we must be able to project in our minds a different picture of our partner and our future together than the one we might well have at the beginning. Anyone *unprepared for change* will not proceed too far down the path of contentment or happiness in relationships.

There is certainly a sense in which the past is lamented by our respondents: they express a recognition that 'being in love' *was* exciting, but *was* a thing of the past and that mature relationships - like wine - become deeper over time, and better. Certainly *different*. Again we must stress that these long-term relationships are only for those able or prepared to change. Which brings us to a slight difference with the genders over the aforementioned issue, albeit evident only in a minority of men:

Female: 'Being in love can be *selfish* and loving someone is a very *unselfish* emotion.'

Male: 'Being in love is a *consuming emotion* but loving someone can be a temporary affair.'

If one was a doctor, one would not necessarily give the above couple an optimistic prognosis for a long, agreeable and fruitful relationship.

Another male expressed a view divergent from the majority: **'Loving someone is tiresome, a 24-hour job, and not one to be in, whereas being in love is.'** In relation to this, when someone mentioned working at relationships it *tended* to be women. Not wishing to draw early conclusions, it is nonetheless evident to me that even in these most basic of issues, communication problems exist, even in couples who express contentment. 'Perhaps men take love and falling in love less seriously than women do?' The response to this question was revealing, if somewhat predictable:

Female: 'Of course men take falling in love seriously, when they get out of the 'impressing' people stage.'

Male: 'No men don't take it seriously.'

This man's views were not particualrly representative of the average male view, although many men felt unable to be seen to be committed to the ideal of love as much as their partners were. Presumably part of their 'impressing' people, for some of them, amounted to a macho denial in the importance of love. A more representative couple were the following:

Female: 'Men take it as seriously but aren't as romantic as women.'

Male: 'Some men are just as serious about it as women are.'

However not all women agreed that men *were* as serious, especially, the older women in the survey. Perhaps they observed something over time that the younger women had yet to experience? However it would be wrong to be jaundiced over the matter. Both men and women tended to view men as being equally interested in love as women are claimed to be, even if many men either are reluctant to say so or do not know their own feelings:

Female: 'My man takes love seriously.'

Male: 'Many men do not until they meet the right one. Sadly many do not give themselves the chance.'

Perhaps the issue is really about the inability of one partner to express what they truly feel, or believe. *How* important is communication between partners of a relationship? How do the partners themselves see it?

We are continually informed that almost all problems within relationships are either *caused* by difficulties of communication or can be *cured* by more communication. Most of our couples *talk*. And most of them feel they talk enough. Of course perhaps a more challenging test will come through the passage of time or in moments of crisis. However, having said that, it does appear that the majority of couples are satisfied with this important dimension of their relationship, as a 33-year-old previously divorced policewoman illustrates:

Female: 'We find it relatively easy to talk to one another about all subjects - I must admit I do most of the talking - I'm very talkative by nature whereas my partner is quiet in his manner and is a person of few words. But when something has to be discussed he will talk.'

Her partner, also 33 and previously divorced, agreed and concurred that she did most of the talking. This tends to be the usual case, as another couple - both in their thirties and in professions - once again illustrate:

Female: 'He encourages me to talk and always seems to know when something is wrong. But I talk more, naturally and from *habit* . He is more considered.'

Male: 'My partner talks more and we quite normally discuss our problems, feelings and intimate matters.'

Although the majority of couples claim that their relationship is one of equal communication in terms of conversation, there is a quite sizeable minority of couples who agree that the woman does most of the talking. Of course much of this may well be habit, training, or the result of living up to expectations (or stereotypes). For example many men *are* raised to believe that they are creatures of *action*, not words, or that they *should* be 'stong silent types.' And of course many men may well realize that such views are nonsense but are nonetheless unable or unwilling to step outside the role of living up to the stereotype.

Those psychologists and observers of marriage who claim that more and more women are claiming that their lives are miserable, that their relationships are failing *because* their husbands are 'not talking to them', do not receive much evidence for it here. *However*, not only do individuals have an immense capacity for self-deception, many women may be either too proud to admit such problems or are simply resigned to being in a relationship in which conversation is somewhat limited.

Indeed most of us are raised in families where both our intimate, personal problems, and our disappointments and crises are invariably dealt with by our **mothers** who tend to be our confidantes more than our fathers. So as partners in the new families we create, it is likely that the woman, the wife, the mother, will do most of the talking. And expectations can easily lead to resignation: a belief that things are unlikely to change.

If we focus specifically on the 'expression of feelings' as an indication of communication, there certainly does appear to be a slight difference between the sexes. Although the majority of people in our survey - both men and women - claim that they do express their feelings when necessary, a quite sizeable minority of couples demonstrate a difference in the sexes. This couple, in their early twenties, are a case in point:

Female: 'I tend to hold in my feelings but I *really really* do try and express them. If I don't I just have a good cry to release tension.'

Male: 'Hold them in - I have always been like this.'

Of course such a tendency to express or suppress feelings is not a static thing. Not only that, but one of the major functions of relationships - indeed what we ourselves hope to get from them - is to add something to our individual lives to make us whole, so it is no surprise that some couples point to such tendencies:

Female: 'I express them probably more than I should.'

Male: 'I have a tendency to suppress my feelings but since meeting my partner I have been letting them out more.'

There is absolutely no doubt that the feminist clarion call to women *and* men that women should not be reduced to domestic servants or restricted solely to the reproductive arena, has had an effect. Women generally speaking *are* more vocal in their rejection of lives of an extremely traditional nature: taking care of the kitchen and the cradle; although it also does have to be said that some women do enjoy such lives and do *not* see them as restrictive. Like most women, most men *have* heard the feminist call to arms, although it equally has to be said that a substantial number of men have found it difficult to change *their* lives substantially enough to help bring in a new dawn of equal relationships in the home. Domestic chores are a case in point:

Female: 'I do most of the housework.'

Male: 'We share the housework.'

Or:

Female: 'Shared.'

Male: 'Seventy-five per cent her, twenty-five per cent me.'

The above responses are typical. Indeed a general trend can be seen in which it appears that a) the woman admits to doing the majority of the housework while her partner refutes this fact, either because he is guilty of his neglect or he simply is unaware of how much housework there is to do, or b) the woman attempts to over-value her partner's contribution out of kindness (pity?) while he may well be more truthful over the matter.

Generally speaking - despite the increase of women in the labour force, the invention of easy-to-operate domestic appliances, and the calls for equality - the tradition remains that women do more around the home, as they have done for centuries.

Attitudes expressed towards feminism itself were interesting. The majority of *both* men *and* women, *spoke* well and encouragingly of the movement and set of beliefs:

Female: 'Yes I think I demand much more out of men and much more of myself. I've always thought women better than men anyway, now I can have the chance to prove it. I'm much more confident. I asked men out - asked them to go to bed with me. Been able to speak more openly and go to places that men think you shouldn't go.'

Male: 'Basically a good thing. Shame about the extremists causing discredit.'

On the other hand a quite small minority of couples both men and women, equally - expressed negative, even hostile views, as in the case of the following 38-year-old woman:

91

'I seem to have spent the last 10 years trying to convince people around me that I really do think feminists are a pain in the derriere and I really do want to be a wife and a mother. And its not that I've been brought up believing a woman's place is in the home - I think its because my mother worked when we were children that I feel the way I do.'

In a similar vein the majority of couples expressed the view that financial matters within relationships ought to be based on principles of equality and indeed were so in their own, and furthermore that financial matters - especially lack of money - *could* lead to tensions, stresses and strains. However a small minority of couples expressed a belief in a more traditional demarcation of roles:

Female: 'Tony is the breadwinner and I stay at home. When I moved in with him I gave up my family income support and one parent benefit because I was no longer entitled to it. Sometimes I wish I had money of my own but we seem to do OK. All the bills get paid and that's the main thing. I know that if I wanted a job he wouldn't stop me so I guess we are happy just as we are.'

Male: 'The lack of it does cause a lot of worries and can lead to tension and possible arguments.'

Children

There is a perceptive old saying along the lines of 'when young, children make your arms ache; when they are older they make your heart ache. Certainly the arrival of children into a relationship changes it so that it will quite be the same again. Some couples appear to embrace the new addition to their circle with ease, with grace. Others struggle, or are torn asunder. And it has been many years since it was *generally* held that we *had* to stay in love less tormented marriages, 'for the sake of the children'. We have learned too much from child psychology not to realize that a loveless cold family life can do more harm to the child than the good a divorce may do; even in the knowledge that such a divorce will also mean a separation for the children. We may well feel that the pendulum has swung too far and that divorce where children are involved is too easy to obtain, but that is another issue we will turn to later. However, the immediate question is, do people believe any longer that children may 'hold a marriage together?'

Not surprisingly *age* is a variable here. For an ex-widow of 60 years of age 'it did for me and my late husband,' - while her new ex-divorced husband, also 60, concurred: 'it should do, but doesn't often happen'.

Overall the view, especially among the younger couples, is that children may create marital difficulties for their parents - unwittingly or otherwise - and should not be the reason for a couple to continue in a relationship against their will or better judgement. Incidentally it is very evident from those in the survey who have experienced it that only a tiny minority take such family disharmony lightly. Most have suffered it with the pain it inevitably causes.

There are, once more, differences between the sexes on the matter. The following two couples - both in their thirties, and previously unmarried - exemplify the difference:

Female: 'Children can drive a couple apart especially if one doesn't want them.'

Male: 'Children won't drive a couple apart.'

And:

Female: 'Children don't hold a marriage together, they often break it up.'

Male: 'Children hold marriages together.'

This diversion of opinion was quite common. Why should it be so? We believe it to be part of the process whereby women are encouraged - and perhaps partly find it 'natural' - to be more concerned in the mechanics of family life than their partners. After all they *do* have the major responsibility for childcare in the home, especially with regard to the *minuitae* of family life. So, by virtue of them being less involved, *men* simply know less of what is going on in their families and have less understanding of the strains brought about by children.

Most in the survey claim they rarely lose their tempers with their children, and generally express positive feelings towards them. This is hardly surprising: admitting that we lose our tempers with our children is a dangerous affair. However if there is a general difference on this matter between the sexes, once more it is the women who state that they do in fact occasionally lose their temper. As they shoulder the majority of childcare duties this is hardly surprising.

Interestingly, when it comes to the older members of the survey, those whose children are 'grown up' and have left home, another pattern emerges. This pattern while not all-pervasive is nonetheless quite significant. Put briefly it is that these older parents do not particularly like being with their children. Do not enjoy or desire such encounters too much.

We should not be surprised at this, but should applaud their honesty. Throughout our lives our image of 'being a parent' is that of caring for babies and young children; when, although such childcare is physically tiring and often without meaningful conversation, at least we feel *we* are shaping *their* lives. However once our children become more and more in control of their own lives, often in ways of which we disapprove, it is all too clear to us that our importance in their lives is in decline. Indeed often our children turn out to be a great disappointment to us, even if they themselves are happy with their own lives.

Another statistical pattern, and one in which lurks many potential problems, is that of the prevalence of 'stepchildren', so called, in families. Take for example the account offered below by a couple, both previously divorced and both well into their thirties:

Female: 'I have none of my own children, but my partner has two by his previous marriage ... I would like a child, but my partner has had a vasectomy and so I have resigned myself that now I will not have children - it causes no problems, no rows, he told me when I first met him ... I do not interfere - he sees his children once a month with me, I get on with them but leave it all to him.'

Male: 'I have two children, a daughter of five and a boy of four. Both from my previous marriage, and now in custody of my ex-wife ... My partner loves seeing my children, whom we visit once a month. My children also enjoy seeing her ... when we spend the weekend with them I possibly give them more *attention* than if I had them full time ... I tried to keep my previous marriage together for my children but it was impossible ... I tried not to have rows in front of the children whilst married to their mother, though occasionally did ... I am close to my children, under the circumstances, though not as much as if I was bringing them up and caring for them ... I like being with *my* children, but not other children really.'

The account of this couple is representative of the average view. Such relationships are a little sensitive, tentative and in which both parties have to tread carefully.

Some couples in our survey do express the feelings that either their partners put their children before they themselves, or that they feel left out of the family's life. When it comes to step-families in particular, some individuals also feel left out, or disapprove of how their partner is rearing their children but not being the 'natural' parent feel unable to interfere.

Overall the existence of children within the relationship appears to be a welcome and manageable state of affairs. We get the impression that although the majority of couples would not stay together in an intolerable relationship solely for the 'sake of the children', nonetheless the existence of children in their lives makes them try a little harder. It is also clear that women tend to shoulder the majority of childcare and, not surprisingly, know more of the secrets involved in growing up.

The relentless increase in the formation of step-families may well result in a number of quite different outcomes. As such family units become more prevalent, individuals will learn more about what is expected of their behaviours within them. Should they feel free to be physically close to their stepchildren, for example? Most importantly, as such developments become more and more natural - and widespread - it will affect how children themselves begin to look at what family life is all about. In the same way that a child growing up in a single parent family may well in their future years desire to live their lives in an alternative way - two parents, a dog, child, roses around the door - or alternatively simply not expect *any* relationship to work out. Similarly stepchildren may well have quite different views as to what constitutes 'family life'.

Perhaps all we can safely say is that whatever degree of emotional hurt such children carry forward into their adult lives, they are also potentially in possession of a *realism* about the *fragility* of human relationships. Despite what we read as children in the fairytales, relationships are brittle, difficult to live through and do not always have happy endings. *Perhaps* stepchildren are better placed than most children to recognize that reality.

Of our survey only a small, although not insignificant, minority expressed the view of *not* wanting children in their lives. Most of the said minority were both honest and 'responsible' in their reasons for such a reluctance:

Female: 'I'm not the "mothering" sort.'

Male: 'I consider it a great responsibility and commitment to bring children into this world and feel neither the inclination or the qualification to do so.'

And:

Female: 'I've never wanted any of my own. I'm far too selfish to devote the time they need.'

Male: 'Never really liked them.'

As we might well have predicted following our earlier discussion as to the definition of and meaning of love, sex itself is seen as extremely important in relationships, in the same way that love and sharing are. Very few in our survey run the two into one: love and sex are seen as quite different aspects to relationships:

Female: 'The sexual side of a relationship is very important. So many relationships suffer when this aspect of a relationship fails - talking helps, which many men can't or won't do.'

Male: 'Sex is very important, though not the be all ...'

Similar opinions were expressed by a couple in their twenties, previously unmarried:

Female: '*Sex is important,* but *trust* and *sharing* is more important.'

97

Male: 'Sex is important but not the be all and end all.'

Another couple, he in his forties, she in her thirties, both previously divorced, acknowledged the importance of sex, but again only in relation to other aspects of a relationship:

Female: 'Sex is very important, but only because everything else is absolutely right. There is trust, there is intimacy, there is commitment, there is fun.'

Male: 'The sexual side is very important.'

In general terms our survey reveals that sex *is* important, but only if everything else in the relationship is satifactory. Love and trust also have to be present for sex to flourish.

Given the above it is therefore hardly a surprise that many individuals complained of having been forced to have sex against their will in *previous relationships* , with men complaining almost as much as women. In response to the question 'have you ever had sex against your will?', a few women talked of being raped, but many more talked of forced sex within previous relationships - a complaint, as we have said, aired by both women and men:

Female: 'Yes, when previously married, many times.'

Male: 'Yes during my first marriage, when I was really too tired or upset, but I felt I should avoid trouble.'

There were, however, some tragic examples of unwelcome sex, as in the following case of a 30-year-old secretary:

Female: 'Whilst living abroad I went for a drink with another boat dweller and he took advantage of me, having plied me with wine. I wouldn't say it constituted rape, just taking unfair advantage

due to the unexpectedness of it. Either way I ended up with *herpes* and now *self hatred*.'

A small minority of men made the spurious claim that it was in fact quite impossible to force a woman into having sex against her will. However perhaps the truly average statement on the matter is best exemplified by the following 41-year-old, previously unmarried, teacher:

Female: 'I've not really ever had sex against my will. I haven't always been 'in the mood', but sometimes I've said 'yes' to please my partner.'

Such admissions, although perfectly understandable in the context of wanting to make our partners happy or wanting to avoid disagreements, are nonetheless disturbing. Rape has its origins *somewhere*: it is therefore absolutely essential, even within the intimate, private and even secretive circle of our relationships, that our profound and inalienable right to say 'no' is both exercised and respected.

Differences between the genders on issues of sex do emerge: overall men stress the importance of sex within relationships slightly more so than women; and, again only by a small margin, more women than men complain of enduring sex against their will.

The majority of couples claim they only indulge in 'normal sex,' with both partners taking turns in being either dominant or subordinate partners. Similarly most couples claim their sex lives are 'normal' - meaning intercourse about twice a week. Another quite regular response is that their sex lives can go weeks, even months in a dormant phase, then change to one of almost constant sexual activity.

The stereotyped belief that it is predominantly males who are interested in sexual paraphernalia, like soft-porn videos or explicit magazines, does not appear to have too much substance. The majority of our survey claim not to be too interested in such items;

99

however the sizeable minority who *do* so consist as much of women as men. For instance in response to the question 'do you enjoy, at all, sexy books or videos?', a previously unmarried couple in their twenties responded:

Female: 'I like sexy books and videos. I would really like to see more.'

Male: 'Sometimes for a laugh.'

To some people soft-porn videos are quite grotesque, and we may well wonder why they are viewed by so many *couples*: the reasons presumably are quite simple. Couples either watch them to stimulate sex between them, to satisfy sexual needs unmet by their partner, or to encourage their sexual fantasy lives. They may, in other words, be an addition to their *real* sexual lives. What about *real* additions to their sexual lives - the committing of adultery for example?

Nobody in the survey admitted to current adultery. In a sense this is quite understandable. Our couples believe they are presently in happy, fruitful relationships, and probably have not felt any impulse to engage in an extra-marital sexual life. Besides that, despite the confidential nature of the survey, the majority of individuals presumably would not wish to admit to adultery; regardless of its actual prevalence, adultery is nonetheless still conceived of as a 'sin' within our western cultures.

Time will determine what percentage of our survey will eventually commit adultery, which some doubtless will do.

The majority of our survey were absolutely adamant in response to the question 'do you ever look for, (and find) sexual fulfilment outside your relationship?, that *no* they didn't. Usually the single word 'no' was used in response. Affairs though are, nonetheless, complicated and often treacherous

100

matters. A previously unmarried 20-year-old clerk and her technician husband express, perhaps unwittingly, how close faithful relationships are to unfaithful ones:

Female: 'I believe that if you are truly *committed* to someone then you should not sleep with anyone else. Although I had an affair with a married man I actually got rid of a boy I was seeing at the time, because I could not sleep with someone as well as sleeping with someone else.'

Male: 'I still eye up girls as most men do, but do not actually look for another relationship.'

Again, not unexpectedly, the majority of our survey claimed they were not worried about their partner being unfaithful, because 'they are not going to be'. Such optimism and positive thinking is understandable and presumably constructive. However our couples *are* aware of what adultery, or unfaithfulness, might well do to their relationship:

Female: 'I think it would shatter him.'

Male: 'I would expect the full wrath.'

A more frequent reply suggests that couples would *understand* their partner's adultery, but nonetheless would find it difficult to *forgive*. Two previously divorced teachers in their forties express this particular point of view:

Female: 'I think he might 'understand' but he would be deeply hurt.'

Male: 'She'd *understand* all right, but she wouldn't like it one jot.'

In keeping with the predictable pattern, the only marginal difference on this matter between the sexes suggests that women may well be more 'understanding' than their partners. This is a reflection of the fact, presumably, that in our cultures it is indeed the men who *tend* to be more unfaithful than women - witness the higher percentage of women divorcing men than *vice versa*. By the same token our western cultures do, sadly, inculcate in men a belief that unfaithfulness by their partners is a terrible slight to their manhood, their sexuality - a devastating blow.

The shift from physical attraction to active sexual relations came surprisingly quickly for the majority of our couples - given that the past decade has been one in which the dangers of herpes and AIDS have been more than spelled out. Some couples waited 'a month or so', while others had intercourse on their first date. For most couples it was a matter of *weeks*. A clerk in her twenties, previously single, explains her strategy, one which her partner, also previously single and in his thirties, did not recognize:

Female: '... the second night. He came back to my flat and I seduced him. I found it quite sweet that although he is 9 years older than me he had no idea I was in fact seducing him and had no idea that I had planned it all.'

Male: 'On the second day. I didn't push things but a month afterwards she told me she'd seduced me. I loved that because women act so subtly and I just didn't realize it even though it's obvious to me now.'

Many couples expressed a view that they decided to engage in sex once they had 'decided to make a go of things and not pursue other dates'; very few individuals were virgins (male or female) in these relationships. The majority in our survey were sexually experienced, with some having been in numerous sexual relationships, others in one or two only - this applied especially to the older members of the survey, brought up in a different moral climate - and such trends demonstrated very little difference between the sexes.

The majority of people remembered their earliest sexual experiences very well indeed:

Female: 'I felt really sick when I first started dating because I thought boys only wanted sex. My first kiss was horrible, I think the boy was trying to eat me. When I lost my virginity the whole thing lasted about 5 minutes, and I remember thinking "'is that it?"'

Male: 'Started dating at about the age of 9 or 10, but once I moved to secondary school was alone and rejected by my school "friends", and never really made good friends since. I first had sex at the age of 22.'

Indeed many women in particular expressed disappointment at their first sexual experience:

'I felt very *risqué* but somewhat disappointed when I first had sex. I discussed boys avidly with my contemporaries and superficially with my mother.'

An older couple point to the reality that sex brings with it all sorts of profound and often confusing emotions. Both of them are in their sixties and widowed:

Female: 'I felt very awkward as I was a very shy person. I thought it was nice, that's all. I cried after I first had sex as I felt mixed up with my feelings. I did not tell anyone...when I first dated John [current partner] I was also quiet and shy. When he kissed me I felt so happy, and when we first had sex I thought I'd burst with happiness.'

Male: 'When I first had sex I felt so awkward. I was embarrassed as both my first wife and I were virgins.'

It is extremely difficult to create a fulfilling relationship if we are constantly making comparisons with previous encounters - earlier marriages for

103

example. We all know of people who never seem to rid themselves of painful memories which impinge upon their newer efforts to achieve happiness. So it is therefore not surprising that for the majority in our survey their *current* sex lives are more satisfying than previous ones. The women of our survey tended to stress the differences in more *qualitative* terms than the men who *tended* to see such changes in more black and white terms:

Female: 'I thought sex was just 5 minutes, but now my current partner has shown me how to enjoy sex and makes sure that I get pleasure as well as him.'

Male: 'Current sex is the best.'

Perhaps one of the clearest examples of the differences in which men and women express their perceptions over different sexual partners is contained in the account offered by the following couple: both in their thirties, both previously single, both in professional occupations:

Female: 'More *intimate* and *honest*, but less *dramatic* and exciting. Sometimes very intense because it expresses real care not just *sexual* desire.'

Male: 'By far the most satisfying and enjoyable.'

This couple truly exemplify a number of realities pertaining to the sexual sphere. To begin with, such sexual relationships are clearly prone to *compromise* - her current partner's sexuality is more intense, more honest, but less dramatic, less exciting. And such a compromise is worth embracing because she perceives her current sexual relationship as reflecting real *love*.

So sex *is* important, *does* express a range of emotions and feelings, is a companion to love, but if practised outside of an ongoing marriage (or other relationship) can lead to bitter recriminations. But as

104

the majority of our survey put it, certainly it is worth having when it is 'good' and within the context of love, but it is *not* love, and not *as* important; though clearly it is nevertheless a crucial ingredient to successful relationships.

What perhaps may be said in conclusion, is that sexual partners are *different* both in terms of what they themselves bring to a relationship and how they affect us, and our sexuality. Some are more experienced, some are more tender, others far more 'exciting', and so on. The partner who turns out to be the most compatible one depends on *our* needs, *our* sexuality and our partner's sexuality, in combination with their other qualities. So we cannot help but conclude that restricting ourselves to only one partner - as some of us do - can only be short-sighted, and perhaps goes some of the way in explaining why so many people appear unhappy or unsatisfied in their relationships.

Has the onset of and publicity given to AIDS made any difference to the sexual lives of our survey?

The majority admit that AIDS *does* concern and worry them, and tend to view it as an epidemic of enormous proportions. They are less concerned *personally*, however, as most of them believe it will not affect them, will not spread to them, that their behaviour is somehow safe and will protect them. Indeed many individuals do talk of sticking only to one sexual partner and of taking precautions. A checkout cashier, previously divorced and in her thirties, as is her partner, puts the general view well:

Female: 'AIDS must be the most important thought when you enter a new sexual relationship, and precautions must be used (condoms) at all times.'

Male: 'If we split up and I met someone else condoms must be used if sex is involved.'

Some individuals have indeed changed their sexual behaviour, while others reflect anxiously and guiltily on their past sexual experiences:

Female: 'AIDS does concern me - and when I think of my late twenties - I know that I would have behaved differently if the same epidemic was there. I would only have had a one to one relationship and not numerous partners.'

Male: 'I am concerned and have changed my views.'

Other individuals are concerned enough to think in terms of being AIDS tested, as has this 24-year-old previously divorced 'housewife':

'When I first heard about AIDS I was very worried but was happy because I was married at the time, and thought nothing of it. When we split up I got worried. Then I met Tony [current partner] and I got to know him and realized he was for me. We haven't had a test for AIDS but we feel that judging from our pasts it was not necessary.'

Male: 'Yes it does concern me but my sexual behaviour has never put me at risk.'

It would be wrong to be totally optimistic about the responsible picture being painted. Clearly on a national level all sorts of individuals clearly do *not* practise 'safe sex', as the rise in heterosexuals being diagnosed HIV Positive is testimony to. And while the majority of the people in our survey are aware, careful and responsible, some still remain somewhat casual in their attitude, if not their behaviour. For example, note the difference in attitude between this couple, in their twenties, both previously single, he being an engineer, she a clerk:

Female: 'AIDS does concern me but I've never been one to sleep around anyway. I haven't changed my sexual behaviour because of it but I'm certainly scared of who I sleep with.'

106

Male: 'I think AIDS is vastly exaggerated for the heterosexual. It concerns me slightly, more so because I am going to work in Saudi Arabia. My sexual behaviour won't change, and my views on sex have not changed because of AIDS.'

Choosing a Partner

Perhaps the most important question put to members of the survey was: 'In choosing a partner and making a relationship work how important do you consider - compared to each other - the following: physical attraction/sex; personality; interests/values; 'character' (like being 'considerate', for example)?'

swering of it - not only because of the mental juggling involoved, but also because the various elements mentioned *are* indeed difficult to weigh up against each other. At certain times one element does seem more important than others; often they seem deeply complementary; age and time makes some more important than others which may well become redundant, and so on. Therefore the average initial general response of 'they are *all* important' comes as no great surprise.

It is also hardly worth repeating the truism that the initial ecstatic sensations of love (and 'sexual love') that many of us feel in the early stages of our relationships simply *cannot* last for ever. Indeed in the definitions of love offered earlier many people talk of love 'settling down'. Therefore it is also no surprise that the elements people look for in choosing long-term partners take into account the changing nature of relationships. Or at least we hope they do.

There are minor differences in this matter between the sexes and as we saw in an earlier chapter some men *can* be seen to be a little more concerned about physical attraction than women. But such men are not widely in evidence. However, the following 30-year-old male is representative of such a minority view:

Male: 'I rate physical attractiveness very highly (perhaps because I want to look good to others with an attractive girl on my arm). Sex is not really an initial priority but will cause friction later on if imperfect. Personality and character I regard as the same thing and take time to show themselves.'

His partner, on the other hand, rated physical attraction as of only 15 per cent importance as opposed to, for example, personality which she thought was of 50 per cent importance in the equation.

It would be reassuring to believe that we might well be initially *attracted* by someone's physical appearance, but that we make serious choices as to partnership on more lasting and serious qualities like personality. However too many individuals clearly hook into a relationship - even become embroiled permanantly in such matters as parenthood - because of physical attraction, *before* they give themselves any real time to make a more rational choice. Besides, making a choice of partner on such superficial grounds as physical appearance - which may in any case change dramatically over time - rules out of consideration people who may well be far better suited to us, if given the time to become acquainted.

However we are not all similar to the previously quoted 30-year-old male. For example many couples rank personality and character in first place, followed by interests and values, and finally, of least importance, physical attractiveness and sex.

Many couples express the reality that *time* alters the order of things, as example the following couple in their thirties recognize:

Female: 'Physical attraction is always the first thing, and it's only when you get to know someone that personality really counts. Its also good to share a common interest.'

Male: 'I consider them all equally important.'

Many individuals express an understanding of the complementary nature of the elements: 'physical attraction is important at first, but if personality is weak this wears off.' Perhaps the opinion most regularly subscribed to is one similar to the following expressed by a 31-year-old, previously single, female insurance clerk:

Female: 'I think you have to find someone with a compatible personality and character. Physical attraction and sex come later. It is an added bonus if you have similar interests.'

This makes considerable sense. We may hypothesize that a normal relationship begins from an appreciation of another person's physical appearance and personality - or at least our first impressions of it. If we still like what we see and hear, we move to touch, to sexual relations. And then as the years take their toll, similar interests may well bolster a flagging relationship. This is not to say that *no* relationships live continually in ecstasy or with a high degree of untainted compatibility, as inevitably some do. Rather it is merely to point out the crucial importance of the passing of time in the success or failure of relationships.

Time itself is used as evidence by our couples in their perceptions of whether their own *parents' marriages* were happy. When we set out to choose a partner we have a mental image of the perfect partner for us. Part of this image originates, as we have previously noted, from our own experiences of living within our families: from our specific relationships with our mothers and fathers. If we are a child of a single parent family, we may seek a supposedly 'normal family life' of two adults, two children, with all the trimmings, or indeed we may seek a similar role in life as a lone parent. Or if we have lived our childhood lives in a fragmented, argumentative and loveless family environment, we may determinedly seek to avoid a repeat pattern in our adult lives. Or we may consciously or unwittingly repeat it: copy the roles we had observed as children. Our survey members tend, in the main, to claim that their own parents had reasonably happy marriages, and define such happiness often in terms of *their parents' years* together. Take the example of the following couple: she, a 41-year-old previously *single* teacher, he a 45-year-old, formerly *divorced* teacher:

Female:'Yes they had a happy marriage. They celebrate fifty years this month.'

Male: 'I think this is difficult. They've been married 46 years and are in many ways *incompatible*. **But they're together; they've lasted.'**

So both the above sets of parents have been married a lengthy time: half a century's worth of conjugal relations. Perhaps *her* parents are equally incompatible, but she is incapable of recognizing it or unprepared to see it. Perhaps *his* parents are *not* incompatible, but his judgement of them is at fault. *Perhaps* he *is* able to see the reality of his parents' incompatability because of his *own* divorce; it may have enabled him to spot some of the clues. It is so very difficult to know the truth of the aforementioned marital maze.

If we can recognize a general trend it is that there is a *slight* tendency of those whose own parents had divorced, to later themselves suffer divorce. What *can* be safely claimed, however, is that those whose parents had divorced were far more perceptive in their reading of the dynamics of their parents' relationships. Again, no surprise. To begin with, their own lives would have been so affected by such a divorce (and previous possible disharmony) that they themselves, not unnaturally, would have taken a considerable interest in such matters. Moreover such an experience would have clearly focused their minds, especially if they were determined to avoid a similar fate themselves. Besides, we all learn, or *should* learn, from our mistakes or from those of others. Living through a divorce as a child (as well as an adult) will inevitably sharpen an individual's powers of understanding the male-female patterns of communication. If, on the other hand, our parents are continually happy, what can we learn from that?

The following couple, both in their forties and both previously *divorced*, are an example of the perceptive observer:

Female: 'My parents were married for 30 years, but they eventually became like *brother* and *sister*, and then divorced. But they still care for one another.'

Male: 'I feel they had a happy marriage, with lots of shared times. I believe they still love and need each other but find it difficult to communicate.'

The patterns of generational changes in marriage are needless to say, complex. For example a previously single, first-time married clerk, 31 years old, describes her parents' lives as follows:

Female:'Father married twice. First was a disaster. Second good. Mother is on her third relationship.'

Finally the following couple demonstrate both *sadness* and *optimism* through their observations. She was previously single, he had been divorced, both are in their early twenties:

Female: 'I think they were happy when us [sic] children were young, but I know they are not at all happy and they know no love between themselves at all.'

Male: 'They seemed happy but divorced after twenty one years when I was sixteen - I don't remember how I felt at the time. It has worked out very well indeed now as I am closer to both parents who are both remarried and much happier.'

Jealousy

We have already mentioned that it is important for couples not to live in the past, not to constantly compare the sexual performances of current partners with previous partners. Couples have to learn to live in the present. Memories can cripple relationships. As we all know, however, the emotion of *jealousy* itself can be such a painful, debilitating and all-encompassing feeling. These feelings that jealousy can produce may also lead to a whole range of destructive behaviours, including those which hurt ourselves, as well as others.

Most of our couples admitted to feeling a degree of jealousy over previous partners, although the majority felt that such feelings were both under control and actually of minor importance. In some couples the men appeared to be more jealous, while in others it was the women. Overall if there *was* a difference between the sexes, it fell slightly towards more jealous men than women. The following two couples are representative of such differences, the first a couple of previously single 20-year-olds:

Female: 'I'm very jealous. I find myself constantly asking questions about his past girlfriends, what they looked like and what sex was like with them.'

Male: 'I'm not at all jealous. She only had two previous relationships, and they were not very happy ones.'

In the other couple - again in their twenties and both previously single - jealousy was reversed:

Female: 'I was jealous about my partner's previous relationships, but the more he told me about them I felt that they were just meaningless.'

Male: 'I am *very* jealous.'

As with many of the dimensions of relationships, *time* and *age* are important factors.

In the earlier stages of relationships, jealousy is more likely to raise its ugly and painful head - as evidenced by the aforementioned 20-year-olds - when individuals are especially keen to cement their relationships. There might well follow a 'middle period' when the individuals are less concerned with cementing their relationships and subsequently express jealousy less often. Finally in the much later stages of a relationship after we have invested a lot of emotional, sexual and practical energy into it, jealousy could well once again surface as a powerful force.

Much depends, of course, on both the extent and the quality of a partner's previous relationships. Indeed it is not accidental that the divorced in our survey also tend to express a little more tendency towards jealousy than the previously single. Again only a slight tendency:

Female: 'Jealous isn't the word - I see his ex-wife every month when he sees his two children. However I also feel a pang of "why couldn't I have met him earlier, before her?"'

Male: 'I'm not. But if my partner insisted on going into detail about past relationships, I would.'

113

Although most individuals expressed only pain and torment over their feelings of jealousy, those who wanted to use their curiosity about their partner's previous relationships *constructively*, tended to be women. While her partner was 'very jealous', one 37-year-old, a previously divorced shop assistant, commented in the following manner:

Female:'I'm not very jealous of past relationships, but I do like to know why and how these relationships have failed so that I can see if we can avoid the same mistakes.'

Sadly, quite a number of people feel cheated that someone else knew their partners before they themselves did. That their partners had lived, if you like, 'previous lives':

Female: 'Sometimes I'm very jealous. I feel I have missed out on someone's love and affection for many years that someone else had.'

However much such an emotion may be understandable, it is nonetheless so utterly pointless and fruitless. Besides, it over values the past, while undervaluing the present: love and companionship should not be measured so simply. One mere day of a *special love* may well be as meaningful, or as joyful, as years and years of other loves.

Hurting Each Other

All of our couples believed they had met their 'perfect partners', that happiness was with them. Obviously, given the high and ever-escalating divorce rate, some of them are a statistical certainty to one day terminate their relationships. Many of the couples are obviously aware of such possibilities, and indeed many of our couples have already been divorced once (or even twice). So we asked our survey what - other than, say, acts of adultery and violence - did their partners do that 'hurt them, and in turn what did they do to their partner that hurt them?'

Some of the couples certainly felt little was actually *currently* wrong with their relationships. All was, if you like, plain sailing. Other couples appeared to be hurt by seemingly the most innocuous of behaviours.

A young married couple in their thirties had hurt each other in different ways:

Female: 'He failed to let me know he would be late home. I called him by the name of a former boyfriend at an intimate moment.'

Male: 'She called me by the name of her previous lover in bed.'

The following couple, previously unmarried, he 30 years of age, a few years older than his current wife, clearly saw things differently from each other:

Female: 'I think the worst thing is most probably arguing. I *know* everyone argues but I hate it - it really gets me down.'

Male: 'The worst thing she ever did was send me away from her hospital bed when she was very ill, saying that she did not want to see me ... I don't think I have *ever* done anything bad to her.'

Certainly many couples talked about their arguing, but there are no significant trends: some couples argue frequently, while others do not; some men within relationships argue more, in others women do so; some couples find it easy to make up, others sulk either in tandem or individually.

Finally there is the situation in which we feel that our partners either do not take us seriously enough or that they deliberately embarrass or shame us. Such behaviour quite obviously makes individuals lose part of their sense of self-worth, and can only increase difficulties within relationships. Often such behaviour only occurs when partnerships are *already* in trouble. Consider the example of the following couple:

Female: 'The worst thing my partner has ever done to me is made fun of me in front of his friends. The worst thing I've done is laughed and made him feel stupid in front of his family.'

Male: 'I feel I am emotionally 'required' to keep saying 'I love you' but this seems a requirement in all relationships. I feel I *have* to do this; it makes me feel uncomfortable when she keeps on about how I do not express this daily.'

We asked our survey about their previous experiences of broken relationships - how it felt at the time and who they turned to for help (or would do so in the future) and how they tried to recover from such obviously painful disappointments.

Some individuals merely commented that they were glad their previous relationships had failed, otherwise they would not have met their current partners. Others somewhat bitterly reinforced the point by saying that the break-ups didn't 'really hurt', and indeed that they 'were lucky to escape'. Most individuals however were more circumspect, and pointed to the feelings they experienced at the time and the ways in which they had since recovered.

The most frequently mentioned emotion, however, especially expressed by women (but not exclusively so) even when they had been ostensibly an 'innocent partner', was that of *failure*:

Female: 'My marriage broke up because of my husband's adultery. The worst thing to cope with were the feelings of *failure* and *rejection* . Only time and a lot of self-analysis helped...My family are very supportive and I would never go to anyone other than my family for help.'

Male: 'Being lonely. I got over it by the help of my friends and family, and the divorce proceedings made me see the light.'

It is difficult not to be saddened at the situations many people find themselves in, and yet we feel optimistic that such people also have an ability to find a pathway to recovery. Although we are all aware that emotional pain and hurt - whether through rejection, betrayal, or whatever - may well leave permanant traces of such hurt. The following 25-year-old, previously single, woman turned to a friend for help, believing that her family would not help her:

Female: 'The worst thing was he just wanted me for my virginity and I really believed he loved me. A friend let me stay with her and I talked him out of my system. I couldn't turn to my family because they didn't like me.'

Male: 'The best thing was that I initiated the divorce proceedings and so kept my self-respect and actually made a decision and stuck to it...I could rely on my family but I have no friends.'

A number of couples were still helping each other - or one was helping the other - over the pain of previous break-ups. This is not to imply that such people met 'on the rebound', rather that it may well take a long time to heal emotional wounds. Also many couples expressed views tantamount to the implication that problems in their previous relationships had been evident from the start. In other words, that the problem was *not* necessarily produced as the relationship had developed, but that they had clearly mis-chosen in the first place:

Female: 'We broke up because of quite different backgrounds and expectations. Worst was *starting over again*, my *confidence was shattered*. Friends helped. They are nearer in age than my family.'

117

Male: 'My ex-wife had terrible anti-social behaviour. The worst thing was parting from my son and the financial hardships. I got over it by going abroad...[in the future]...I might go to family, but to cousins *not* my mother.'

Many couples spoke of such seemingly extreme solutions - leaving the country, their social lives, their work, and so on. Others on the other hand relied on pharmaceutical or alcoholic help. Many admitted to the healthy avenue of self-examination and the learning in which such a process may result.

If trends did emerge they certainly were the same for both sexes. Feelings of failure were paramount, followed closely by those of rejection and loneliness. In terms of solutions to the situations they found themselves in, the majority of people turned to both family and friends. The small amount of hostility reserved for one or other group tended to be aimed at family rather than friends. Again this is hardly surprising. We tend not to wish to admit failure to our family who may well have been involved in our choice of partner in the first place. Also families, as we know, can be judgemental. Friends on the other hand, at their worst may be pleased we are once more single again and no longer in relationships of which they had disapproved, while at best will remain supportive and non-judgemental.

The two factors of 'time as a healer' and the 'replacement partner' were pre-eminent in most people's minds as the *ultimate*, solutions to the pain caused by the break-up of their relationships. If there were differences between the sexes here they were only marginal ones, and suggested that men may be slightly more likely to look for another relationship a little *earlier* than women. Whether such a strategy is a good one is in fact a matter of dispute between psychologists and, also importantly, a matter of considerable luck.

We cannot underestimate the power we can have over each other, crimes of passion being but one publicly viewed example of such power. As we have seen many couples talked of profound hurt and pain, and of subsequent loneliness. Some also talked of being driven to the contemplation of suicide following the ending of a relationship. So we explored these feelings further, and asked people in our survey whether or not they were ever lonely, even *within* the relationships that they currently hold so dear.

Once again there was little evidence of any difference of opinion on this matter between the sexes, especially in relation to the contemplation of suicide. The following woman in her thirties, and previously divorced, told of her contemplation:

Female: 'I was in love with someone once and we both knew there was no future in it because of vast religious differences. I got as far as suicidal thoughts [and] ...when I was approaching my thirtieth birthday and had no relationship, and felt life wasn't worth living because I didn't have anyone to share it with ... I used to feel lonely because I had no one to share my innermost thoughts with.'

Interestingly her current partner claimed he had rarely felt lonely and had 'never, never *ever* contemplated suicide.' Their relationship *did* appear to be based partly on, or seemed to be a reflection of, some kind of compatability based on *complementary* traits.

A 40-year-old, previously unmarried, male illustrator *also* has felt suicidal:

Male:'I've had a very rough time over the years in relationships. I've considered suicide *seriously*, twice.'

A couple in their early twenties, also both previously single, probably express a view held by the majority of others:

Female:'I have contemplated suicide a number of times. I did so because I couldn't express my feelings ... I've always felt loneliest after a *broken relationship*.'

Male:'I get upset and depressed very easily. I was loneliest from the age of twelve onwards - *my formative teenage years were awful*. I wish I had been more handsome at the time. Yes and I'm still lonely now, even with my present partner. I'm just a loner.'

Others mention specific events such as 'anniversaries' producing a sense of loneliness or despair, or of definite changes in family life; the following 46-year-old, previously divorced, telephonist explains the loneliness she experienced: 'Once my daughter was grown up leading her own life, combined with friends celebrating anniversaries.'

Of course many people possess the ability to 'snap out of it', so to speak, they have the ability to get over their disappointments and get on with their lives: 'I cried myself to sleep after my husband left because I tried not to cry in front of my son. I have never contemplated suicide - *no man is worth it*.'

As we suggested earlier, it was often an individual's new relationship which provided the ultimate solution to their despair and loneliness. Such a solution, of course, is only likely if the partners have the desire and ability to help each other: they must be able to demonstrate a particular degree of compatibility. Take the case of the following couple, she in her thirties, he in forties, both previously single:

Female:'Every man that I have finished with I have cried myself to sleep, because I always

120

thought there would be no other like him or would be so good with me. I got over it in a week or two when someone else came along ... I remember in my early twenties I contemplated suicide because I "loved" him so much ... *I am lonely nearly all the time, even with my partner.*'

Male:'Never contemplated suicide ... *never* lonely.'

So this couple experience quite different emotions: one knows loneliness, the other doesn't. Yet they are in a successful relationship; they feel themselves to be happy. This particular quality of *compatibility* we return to in some detail in the following chapter.

Marriage and divorce

Many of our couples, not surprisingly, felt at their lowest ebb at the ending of marriages, or relationships, because of being divorced. We enquired into our survey's general feelings towards the institutions of marriage and divorce.

Interestingly, a significant minority of the survey saw no *real* difference between marriage and cohabitation. The *majority of such people* believed that marriage was 'but a piece of paper', and that the same degree of commitment was likely (and necessary) in relationships of cohabitation as in marriage. Additionally, they viewed the escape clause of divorce in two quite distinct ways. On the one hand it could make those in a marriage try harder to make such a relationship work because of the heartache and administrative difficulties (including financial ones) that occur with divorce. While on the other hand as divorce *was* a possible alternative to a marriage continuing, many of our survey felt that such a reality stopped people trying harder to make things work - 'if it doesn't work out we'll divorce'.

Cohabitation on the other hand was felt, by those who compared it to marriage, to be as firm a commitment and, moreover, a relationship with no *real* easy escape clause. Meaning that although there were no legal strings attached to cohabitation, and as any partner could theoretically 'just walk away', the psychological reality of the relationship made it unlikely that it would be quite as easy as that.

Despite what has just been said, the *majority* of couples were nonetheless inclined towards marriage as the primary institution. This is quite understandable, considering the cultural and economic pressure in our western societies for us to marry, rather than to live together. Indeed, one of the most prevalent and forcibly argued opinions is that if we are to have children we certainly ought to be married. Again such a view is hardly surprising given the moral and religious bases of our western cultures; nonetheless the national trend of more and more children being born 'out of wedlock' suggests a more complex pattern of actual behaviour.

Not surprisingly, the older members of the survey - and the religious ones also - were more inclined towards marriage than the younger ones. There appeared very little difference between the sexes over both institutions of marriage and divorce.

The following couple, she a 37-year-old previously divorced teacher, her partner 10 years her senior and a manager, also previously divorced, express the widely held views of the survey:

Female:'Marriage is an important public commitment ... to be married is to be faithful, be committed, share joys, sorrows and responsibilities ... Divorce is not wrong, it might well have to be considered. I myself have been through one, my partner has been through one.

122

Now we are together. A divorce is not the end of your life.'

Male:'Marriage *is* an important public commitment ... is about faithfulness, fidelity, trust, no jealousy ... [but] ... There is no point in staying together and making life a misery.'

So there is general and widespread belief in the importance of marriage as both a personal and public commitment to each other. Once more we see the important words *faithfulness* and *trust,* and *no jealousy.* We also find the view widely expressed that divorce may well be the only solution to an unhappy marriage. What is also clear, however, is that for a sizeable minority of the survey - indeed almost the majority - divorce has become too easy an option, and should be made more difficult. This view is held strongly by a considerable number of people whether or not they themselves have been previously divorced: that fact seems to make little difference. The following couple are *both* previously divorced and now in their forties:

Female:'Marriage is *forever.* I don't believe in divorce. Divorce is too easy, and permits people to run away from problems of their own making. I am divorced! When my husband told me he didn't want me any more, I took the opportunity to leave an unhappy marriage. As long as *he* was happy I would have stayed.'

Male:'People consider divorce too easily, resulting in couples not working to save a marriage.'

This next couple on the other hand were previously single, much younger - in their early twenties - yet shared a similar perspective:

Female: 'I don't think people fully realize what is involved in *marriage vows* and they don't work at making a marriage. Society has made divorce too easy and acceptable ... however, if a marriage is

123

completely over then it is more wrong *not* to divorce.'

Male: 'Divorce is too easy.'

A number of couples, and especially the women, mentioned the neglect of marriage vows, while many others talked of the importance of the moral and religious bases of marriage. Nonetheless such expressed opinions were in a minority. For instance very few people shared the opinion of a 29-year-old, previously single, self-defined 'typist', who claimed although she was 'not religious', she absolutely did not 'like the thought of people living together before marriage, or out of marriage'.

Obviously to embark on marriage is a considerable act of courage, given the current high divorce rate. It involves much hope and belief in its permanent possibilities. We wouldn't set out on such a path if we thought otherwise. Most of us are not, however, utterly naive.

Some of the survey, a tiny minority, expressed some rather remarkable thoughts, such as the following 23-year-old male computer programmer:

Male:'Marriage gives a "permanent feeling" to the commitment between us ... [and] ... divorce is completely wrong, as marriage should not be considered in the first place if it is likely to end in divorce.'

Marriages are simply unpredictable encounters and, as we have repeatedly observed, *change over time*.

Divorce signals defeat, failure and often brings on feelings of great pain, despair and in the darkest moments even embraces thoughts of suicide. Financial disaster can also follow, as can excruciatingly painful separations from beloved children. *However*, it would be wrong to simply stress the negative side to all of this. Many of our

124

couples, as earlier reported, argued that divorce was often the only solution. If all else failed it *was* an option. Indeed most of us have presumably experienced claustrophobic relationships in which we have felt more like a prisoner than a lover. And there *is* no other solution to constant, repeated marital disharmony, of strife, failed communication, disloyalty or violence. As a 49-year-old, previously divorced, male security officer put it:

'Divorce is often the only way out. *It releases the sad and the oppressed.*'

Chapter Five:
Coupledom

Who'd a thought we could be lovers.
She makes the bed and he steals the covers.
She likes it neat and he makes a mess.
Oliver Leiber (and sung
by Paula Abdul,
Opposites Attract).

The chorus of Oliver Leiber's song continues, 'I take two steps forward, I take two steps back - we come together because opposites attract.' Over the decades psychologists have not found it quite so easy to put pen to paper on the issue of compatibility to produce fruitful conclusions. We were, however, interested in such matters and asked our survey a number of questions about *compatibility* with their partners. An initial question asked them whether or not their current partner was indeed like the 'man or woman of their dreams?' Was the current partner like the mental picture of their 'perfect partner' they had been carrying around in their head, and which had been guiding them in their search for love?

Female: 'He's not.'

Male: 'Not really. The woman of my dreams is an extremely fertile, small, slim 17-year-old who thinks I'm wonderful, always will, and will produce half a dozen children who wouldn't be any trouble to me ... oh, she'd need the mind and experience of a 50-year-old like me, too.'

Joking apart, the *majority* of our survey did believe that they

had more or less found what they were looking for. In one sense this could well be accurate. For a start there is a degree of a self-fulfilling manipulation at work: meaning, if we do not wish to meet small fat men it is *probable* that we will try and put ourselves in social situations where we can avoid such small fat men. Also once we have decided to settle down with one particular person we not only have to make *compromises* both mentally and practically, we also have to adjust the picture of our 'ideal' partner to the 'reality' of the one we actually have. And before long the two may well begin to look the same. What is more it is not actually helpful to believe that our partner is *not* what we're looking for, and that consequently we have had to settle for second best. Such a feeling is *not* a good start to a relationship.

A couple in their twenties believed their partners were 'virtually a perfect copy', an 'exact copy', of their dreams, while the following couple, also in their twenties, were more circumspect in their reply:

Female:'He is down-to-earth with a good sense of humour - kind and considerate. That means a lot to me - so he *does* bear a resemblance to the "man of my dreams".'

Male:'Very similar.'

Other couples believed their partners were *not* what they had imagined would be ideally suitable for them, but they were, nonetheless, pleased with what they had got:

Female:'Not really like him at all, but really is better.'

Male:'I haven't a "woman of my dreams" really, but I do have her.'

Many of the couples were well aware that their partners were, in a sense, *a compromise* even if only to a degree. We can't *all* meet witty, handsome, wealthy and kind partners, if that is what we want. Indeed living in a relationship necessitates the removal of many illusions (as well as hopes); and compromise sometimes results in disappointment. If there was a slight difference at all in the trends here it had to do with *age* rather than gender, with the older members of our survey appearing - not surprisingly, by virtue of their experience - *at times* a little more realistic about such compromises. The following are a couple in their fifties, the female previously divorced:

Female:'He is not like the "man of my dreams". He lacks an *overt personality* - as a friend said, "he is a bit colourless, but then you are usually surrounded by *very* colourful people". He has, however, all of the qualities that I admire.'

Male:'I do not have a "dream" partner.'

Yet they are *together*. And may well remain so. This situation is perfectly summarized by a 49-year-old, previously divorced, businessman:

Male:'I didn't really have a "woman of my dreams". There has to be *compatibility*, and this is a complex matter.'

This question of what constitutes compatibility is indeed extremely complex and without an easy answer.

Compatibility

As we have recognized, relationships change over time - inevitably. Therefore if we are interested in compatible relationships that last *over time*, one aspect of such compatibility must be a *mutual* ability to change and in ways which please the other partner:

128

or at least in ways, or to such a degree, which their partner can tolerate. This, however, is not something we can investigate here. Only over the years can a relationship be tested and only after time has passe are we able to say *in retrospect* whether or not a relationship possesses genuine compatibility. However, by its very nature compatibility is also about *mutuality* as much as other things, and this is what we asked our survey about.

We asked about mutuality first of all by posing questions concerning *d*ependence, *in*dependence and *inter*dependence.

Not surprisingly the majority (we presume, quite *truthfully*) saw their relationships in terms of interdependence - relationships of mutuality, of give-and-take. Of *sharing*.

Female: 'I like to know I can lean on him. But we are interdependent.'

Male: 'We share.'

The **previously divorced** individuals tend to be a little more expansive about compatibility and such elements as give-and-take, but this is presumably due to a reflection on their previously failed relationships. The following couple in their forties, both in professional occupations, epitomize the point:

Female:'He makes the important decisions after consultation. I'm quite happy about this and I would say so if there was something I disagreed strongly with ... I think we are interdependent and becoming more so.'

Male:'All people who live together successfully should have interdependencies. I do "need" her, but not obsessively so, nor to a dangerous extent.'

There *is* evidence of a difference between the sexes, albeit an exceedingly slight one, and this merely reflects some traditional stereotyped ideas:

namely that the male *ought* to make the 'important decisions' within a relationship and that a woman should feel dependent on her partner. And of course the economic inequalities so evident in our cultures tend to reinforce such ideas. The following couple illustrate the point and also the difficulty some of us appear to have with the notion of interdependence:

Female:'I do like to feel I am dependent on my partner. I think a woman likes to feel secure in a relationship. However my partner tends to depend on me as well.'

Her partner emphasizes the matter somewhat differently:

Male:'I have always valued independence and still do in my relationship now. I tend to think of interdependence as too much of a romantic ideal.'

Indeed, a considerable number of couples emphasized rather different aspects of their relationships, and many contradicted each other's versions as to what went on within their circle of intimacy. A female public relations manager asserted with certainty that her partner 'always makes the important decisions,' while he, like her thirty-something, claimed equally adamantly that 'we always make the important decisions jointly'. This mis-communication afflicts all sorts of couples; for instance the following pair in their early twenties, and both in the catering trade:

Female:'*I* make all the important decisions ... [and] ... we are both very independent people.'

Male: 'We discuss decisions and always come to a mutual agreement ... (and) ... I would like to feel we are dependent on each other.'

Some people appear to be *intuitive* when it comes to matters of love and relationships. *Some* of us handle the ups and downs, highs and lows, and the nuances of partnership much easier than others. *Some* individuals appear to enjoy *all* aspects of relationships, even the crises and disappointments. However, most of us learn only over time, through experience often painful, and often only through previous failures. *Sharing* is a case in point. This interdependence is invariably well-valued, but *is* nonetheless extremely difficult to achieve. Some of us are clearly unable to recognize or achieve it. Some of us deceive ourselves (and our partners) that we have it, when we in fact don't. A few of us seem not to want it. However, generally speaking, experience showed our couples that interdependence (sharing) was the most appropriate relationship for most 'normal' couples, **but additionally that independence and dependence are both** *part of* **interdependence and are also important in their own right.**

The following woman, 46, and previously divorced, demonstrates a knowledge based on such life experience, and summarizes the argument concisely:

Female:'I like to think that we discuss decisions thoroughly, then make them together. I hope he doesn't let me have my way against his own will, even in little things ... [and] ... I like to feel that we are both capable of being completely independent if necessary, also that if ill I could become completely dependent on him and that he could cope with it, *and* **that we both enjoy an interdependent relationship, too!'**

The same woman commented that she *respected* her partner and that he in turn respected her: 'we respect each other as individuals, and he is one of the few men I know who treats me as a person and not as a "mere woman"'.

Being respected by our partner and feeling that we are not 'taken for granted' are the kinds of factors that develop in importance over the life of a relationship. If there are faults in this area they may not be the *precise* cause of marital dissolution, as adultery might well be, but they are the ingredients in a relationship which can quietly, over time, reduce it to a state of being worthless. They are not dramatic ingredients of a relationship, but critical nonetheless.

We often hear people - usually women - complain that their partners take them for granted. Often this refers to the fact that they believe themselves to b333 unfairly burdened with a disproportionate amount of domestic chores. The feeling that we are not 'respected' can mean a number of things, but usually that our 'will' is disregarded, as are our opinions, desires, selves, by our partner; our identities, our personalities are not considered to matter.

Most of our couples believed in the importance of respecting each other and most claimed that they in fact did so. Very few admitted that they didn't, and similarly very few stated that they deliberately took their partners for granted. Frequent comments were of the order that: 'I try not to take him/her for granted ... I try always to appreciate him/her.'

Of course we are not innocent bystanders in these matters. We *can* interrupt the process and say 'stop, please don't take me for granted'; we can insist on being respected: again, yet another aspect of an ability to communicate and an expression of mutuality. For some of our couples, being respected was indeed an absolutely critical part of being in love:

Female: 'I respect him a lot or I would *not* love him otherwise. He does respect me or I would *not* trust him if he did not ... I do not take him for granted - he will *not* let me!'

Being 'respected' usually referred to the survey people's opinions, personalities and decisions being valued and taken into account. Occasionally our survey touched on the more interminate: 'I try to respect him but I don't always consider his desire for "space".' While another couple in their twenties, and both previously single - unusual in the survey - admitted to less than perfect behaviour:

Female: 'Yes, I do take advantage, although I do try not to.'

Male: 'I do respect her in a way but she doesn't seem to have any independent character - she always agrees with what I want to do. I would have more respect if she stood up and demanded things for herself ... I believe she respects me ... Undoubtedly I take my partner for granted, but not in a mean way. I don't "use" her but I organize things for us without consulting her sometimes.'

A 30-year-old marketing manager, formerly single, also believes herself to be less than fully respected and also knows of the pitfalls involved in taking a partner for granted:

Female: 'I *think* he respects me, but sometimes he thinks I'm too "sweet" to respect, especially when I behave in ways he sees as childish ... [and] ... sometimes *I'm* unnecessarily rude and unkind and moody and suddenly realize that he might one day have had enough.'

So what makes them stay together, we might well ask? More generally, what makes people believe they are compatible?

In general the people in our survey, in answer to questions concerning reasons for compatibility and also comparisons made with previous relationships, responded with a list of ingredients: that sex is now better, more shared interests, interesting opposite interests, more communication, a kinder and more considerate relationship, and so on.

133

Many couples believed in the importance of *similar* backgrounds, interests and ways of looking at life:

Female:'We have both had similar ways of life, and been along the same path. We think the same and are on the same wavelength ... I don't have to try so hard at being someone, try to prove myself, make excuses for myself. I am what I am and I can *relax* and enjoy this relationship.'

Male:'Similar backgrounds, and a very full life ... my previous marriage was very physical with little mental awareness. My present relationship is like a breath of fresh air.'

However, there were as many couples who pointed to the importance of the attraction of opposites: 'we are so different that the challenge is exciting'. And there were those couples who appeared to differ on what made them compatible. The following couple are thirty-something, educationally well-qualified and previously single:

Female:'He is the stabilizing balance against my vitality. I livened up his rather staid life. Opposites attract!'

Male:'Similar outlook on life. Similar backgrounds.'

As with the majority of talking points concerning relationships, the women tended to express their opinions more expansively, but otherwise there were few differences on the issues by the respective sexes. *Age,* however, produced a slight difference of emphasis. With increasing age we presumably look for different aspects of a relationship: *desires* remain of course, but are tempered through knowledge and experience. Indeed the older couples of our survey tended to emphasize a little more the importance of shared and similar backgrounds and interests:

Female:'Same age, interests, moral standards, intelligence; similar social class and work status ... and very important is a great tolerance of individuality ... This is the first *sensual* relationship I have had. Here is a good man, one worthy of devotion.'

Male:'Three or four basically similar interests, a similar belief in fairness, and an equality of responsibility.'

Shared values together with a concern about fairness and honesty are not, however, the sole property of the older couples. A 32-year-old, bilingual secretary, previously single, talked of 'sharing the same values and ideas about bringing up children', and that her present relationship was so much better than her failed engagement as she could 'trust her husband totally', and that there were 'no nagging suspicions about his honesty'.

In ranking the importance of various ingredients of compatibility, the ability to *talk* to a partner was considered to be of equal importance as sexual compatibility.

Female:'We get on so well together - we never argue, manage to "communicate" ... my present partner and I talk whereas my ex-husband didn't talk at all.'

Male:'We are willing to come and go with each other.'

Given the fact that divorce is becoming such a commonplace experience in our cultures, it is not surprising that many people find compatible those individuals like themselves who have suffered divorce and been hurt. For many people the sharing of such experiences are necessary and desirable aspects of a new relationship. A man in his forties painfully explained that what makes him and his present wife compatible was the fact that they had both been 'so hurt in the past', and that therefore they both 'make allowances'. He added, incidentally, that he had previously 'given up' the belief that he would find his perfect partner and would 'have settled for less'.

The freedom to be ourselves, to behave in ways which we find comfortable and to be *respected* for what we are, figured highly in some couples' stories:

Female:'This feels so natural ... I am *not* proving anything to anyone as I was in my previous relationship.'

Male:'This time I feel emotionally secure, wanted and loved for *myself* - for what I am and not what I "should be".'

Uncertainty, however, continues to lurk around the edges of our relationships. A 27-year-old hairdresser, formerly single, warmly observes that:

Female:'He is a more considerate and loving man than anyone I've ever known. I feel wanted and appreciated by him, basically also his best friend, something I've never felt with anyone else. I've always felt like just an object with other men.'

Her partner, however feels - presumably unbeknown to her - a little differently:

Male:'I am unsure of the future ... I just don't feel secure.'

The majority of our survey felt that their feelings and thoughts towards their partners were consistent, and rarely contradictory. Individuals *did* talk of arguing, but arguing less about personal matters and more over *issues* both social and intellectual. Others repeatedly stressed that *yes* they did often *compromise*, but saw it as part and parcel of being in a relationship. Others - usually, but not always, women - observed that their *view* of their partner *was* stable, although their feelings were not.

136

Surprisingly a high percentage of people frankly admitted to having a 'history of repeatedly picking the "wrong" man/woman':

Female:'Yes, which is why I no longer trust myself.'

Male:'Not conspicuously "wrong", but certainly not ideal.'

A self-described 'housewife' of 40 years of age gave the matter some thought and on reflection commented that:

Female:'I didn't think so but looking back the man I married was definitely wrong for me, and also my last relationship which lasted 6 years went *terribly* wrong, so yes, I suppose I have had a history of repeated wrong choices.'

But most people were nonetheless convinced that their particular relationship would 'last forever', and indeed many couples talked of 'growing old together'. There were very few differences of opinion between the sexes in this matter, although *age* and prior experience of relationships *did* - not surprisingly - make a difference.

A previous unsatisfactory relationship inevitably will cloud our perceptions and opinions. A 37-year-old, previously divorced policeman commented that he had become a sceptic and, despite a current 'happy marriage', fears accepting the view that it will 'last for ever, as it might lead to another source of grief'.

Other couples entered their new relationships with a 'realism' which, while no doubt pretty accurate, led to a considerable reduction in expectations. And inevitably their relationships would be tinged by such prior experience:

Female:'A divorce has clarified a lot of my thinking. I used to be far too idealistic and not

137

realistic enough - I should not have been surprised
to find that marriage to a semi-literate farmer
didn't work ... [and] ... no relationship of mine
(other than straightforward friendship) has ever
lasted. I expect this one will either grow into
something better than we have now, or fade away.'
Male:'I do not place *expectations* on our
relationship.'

In Search of Love

Oscar Wilde famously, if caustically, commented that
'one should always be in love; that is the reason one
should never marry'. For *our* couples the search for
love *was* the search for a perfect partner, within
marriage or otherwise.

Some talked of the all-encompassing nature of
being in love, of loving and of their relationships in
general. The majority clearly believed that 'love' had
not only improved their lives but indeed was that
which made life worthwhile. Even following a
divorce or another previous disappointment, or an
experience of the negative power of love, people
nonetheless wanted 'love' more than anything else.
A male 45-year-old teacher talked of the
claustrophobic nature of some of the love he had
previously experienced, a 'love' of such power that it
led to the greatest emotional crisis of his life. Perhaps
not surprisingly the same man felt that 'love' itself
had not changed him: 'age has changed me;
experience has changed me'.

The majority felt that love had clearly changed
their lives, and changed *them*, invariably for the
better. The following 50-year-old's experience was
repeated by many others:

Female:'I'm completely happy and would like to help others reach this level of contentment. I consider "us" now, not "me".'

Male:'Love has made me a more caring person.'

In a similar vein others talked of 'love' giving them 'someone else to think about and look after other than themselves', and many talked of a development in their degree of understanding and caring. However the other side of the coin was apparent also: people were fearful of *losing* 'love', and many felt this to such a degree that it made their current relationships unnecessarily stressful. Other couples expressed another fear, namely the 'daunting task of keeping someone's love for years'.

Developing and maintaining a harmonious, fulfilling and compatible relationship is probably the most daunting human task. Compared to it, a step on the moon is a piece of cake. We are constantly urged to 'fall in love' and form a couple, so much so that after a while we believe it to be the only *natural* manner in which to spend our lives. However, we are taught little if nothing about how to achieve such harmonious coupledom.

What coupledom entails is a combination of our qualities and of dependence, independence and interdependence. In other words we have to achieve a balance between being both an individual and part of a relationship willing to compromise, which will be able to change over time.

Very few alternatives, however, were offered to that of 'love' and coupledom, although the following woman demonstrated that *ironically* perhaps one of the best qualities needed to make and survive relationships is the ability to be alone:

Female:'Despite my happiness, love has taken time and energy away from other things, e.g. housework; caused me to see less of friends, to ignore church teaching on fornication, i.e. when it suits me ... [and] ... In the past I was first to fall out of love, twice, and was so upset by hurting the men that it was *I* who on each occasion had the nervous breakdown. I've never been afraid of losing love, even when it happened, as I knew I was strong enough to survive it and live alone.'

PART THREE: LASTING LOVE?

Chapter Six:
What might the future bring?

If the rich are getting richer, it is not by collecting interest cheques, playing the futures market, or investing in tax shelters. It is because millions of women get up and go to the office in the morning.

JOHN NAISBITT

and PATRICIA ABURDENE

The authors of *Mega-Trends 2000* point out that during the 1990s well-educated, skilled information workers will earn the highest wages in history, further reinforcing the decade's affluence. While 1992 will see a Europe without frontiers for its twelve European community members, so that a Greek lawyer will be able to set up a practice in Copenhagen and a Spanish shoe company would be able to open a shop in the streets of Dublin.

Naisbitt and Aburdene believe that in the 1990s the arts will gradually replace sport as society's primary leisure activity. Further on in time - the not too distant future - they talk of a further shift in the trend from broadcasting to narrowcasting. As they put it, video cassettes, tape decks in cars, Walkmans and home CD players 'put the power of the airwaves in one's own hands'. The authors assert that so enthusiastically are we swapping food, music and fashion, that a new international lifestyle reigns in Madrid, Osaka, Seattle and Chelsea. And it is indeed consumer-driven: drinking cappuccino and Perrier; eating sushi; dressing in the United Colours of Benetton; listening to American and British rock while driving the Hyundai over to McDonalds. Harrods fruit and vegetable department stocks French peaches, Dutch radishes, English strawberries, Californian asparagus, Russian button mushrooms, and East African lemon grass. Harrods itself, which operates shops in West Germany and Japan, is owned by Egyptians.

Today one billion passengers fly the world's airways each year. By the year 2000 it will have risen to two billion passengers - even now, every single day three million people fly from one place on the planet to another. 'Dallas' is seen in eight countries, while Mickey Mouse and Donald Duck - their voices dubbed in Mandarin - are seen weekly in China. Meanwhile more than 80 per cent of all information stored in more than one hundred million computers around the world is in English.

What, you may well ask, has this to do with the search for love?

Quite simply 'the future' has a considerable impact on the way in which *we* ourselves live our daily lives *now*; it affects decisions we make for our lives in the future; produces new traditions and cultural norms which may well affect us; and, of course, our children's lives will be greatly changed by 'the future' and what it brings. We have an example of change in our own time: divorce *used* to be frowned upon; was considered undesirable and unwarranted behaviour; *now* it is considered acceptable, so consequently more and more of us do so.

The question is, what changes will the future bring? Perhaps divorce will go out of fashion? Even within *our own individual* lives unexpected changes take place, the effect of which can penetrate to the most personal aspects of our lives.

Predicting the future

So what may the future shape of love, sex, marriage, divorce and the family become? Will we change our patterns of relationships, be affected by different trends and newer traditions?

It is perhaps important to re-emphasize once more the undeniable fact that it is *time itself* which provides the true test of our relationships. Only after a number of years can we truly measure the success or otherwise of our personal partnerships.

The authors of *Mega-Trends 2000* point to at least *two* changes they foresee which will affect our personal relationships. To begin with they predict, on the basis of what they term 'unmistakable signs', the rise of a 'worldwide religious revival'. They anticipate a return to our more fundamental values, concerned specifically with our conduct and behaviour.

Perhaps we ought to say from the outset that *futurology*, as it is sometimes termed, is a quite difficult art, certainly prone to unreliability. Indeed one of the few certainties we *can* make of the future is that it is, in fact, *un*certain. However, *changes* there will be, and it does little harm to attempt a prediction as to what shape they might take. Besides, some changes have already begun, and what is at issue is simply their future rate of growth and possible new shape.

There indeed does appear to be some kind of renaissance of religious or, more accurately, spiritual ideas. The growing interest in so-called 'New Age' ideas being a case in point. Similarly the concern over 'green issues' certainly has spiritual undertones. Any spiritual changes which may occur could affect our personal, intimate lives in a number of ways. Perhaps most important are the following two implications.

With *any* religious revival comes an emphasis on the *individual* - so individuals themselves are responsible for their salvation. Individuals are invariably held accountable for their destiny. Indeed the aforementioned authors go so far as to assert the developing importance within *our* culture of the more eastern notion of *Karma* - as you sow, so shall you reap; every action generates consequences which we will eventually face.

Certainly this emphasis on the individual, on our *selves*, could well result in individuals thinking more about their lives, their true desires and goals, and also their *conduct*. Which leads us to the second implication, namely a possible reconsideration of our moral codes.

Not many of our survey admitted to any great degree of religious feelings or commitment. Most, like the nation at large, were somewhat indifferent to its role in our lives. However those who *did* express a religious commitment talked of such matters as the importance of marriage vows, life-long marriage, and of their disapproval of the ease of divorce. So we could well expect *any* religious revival to re-emphasize those considerations for a greater number of people.

The other major change - already *well* in train - which may well affect our personal relationships concerns the constitution of the labour force. For the authors of *Mega-Trends 2000* the 1990s and onwards will be a period of 'women in leadership', as they put it. They point out, statistically, that for the last few decades in the USA, for instance, women have taken two thirds of the millions of new jobs created each year in the 'information technology' sector. This, the authors add, they will continue to do both in the US and elsewhere.

This change has already begun, as we have previously indicated. And as we are all aware, the stresses and strains, dilemmas, balancing acts and tensions involved in being a working woman *and* a partner (and especially a mother also) are of considerable importance in determining the degree of success and fulfilment of personal relationships. Indeed it may be the case that for the past three or four decades in the western world, the rise of the working woman has been the single most important factor in the changes observed in the life-long struggle/bargain between the sexes. The changing responsibilities of childcare, a changing economic climate within the family, and the broadening of a woman's social environment, are *all* brought about by women's increasing involvement in the labour force which has *radically* altered the balance between the sexes.

It is, of course, a *generational* phenomenon. Our father's father would not have dreamt of a world in which marriage consisted of a sharing of domestic responsibilities and an equality of financial involvement. Similarly our father's daughters - women of today - would, in the main, expect a greater equality in relationships than they observed in their mother's role. Indeed perhaps it is even possible to claim that the tendency - usually attributed to women - to want to balance the top priorities of career and family without losing out on other personal interests, is in fact generational, and *not* gender-specific. *Not* attributable *only* to women.

Whether or not a continuation of these quite radical - in the sense of a comparison with the pre-1950s world - changes will increase the tensions in our personal lives as we attempt all sorts of balancing acts, or whether we begin to satisfactorily *adjust* and

146

change our behaviours accordingly, simply remains to be seen.

The Future of the Family

As we have noted in our earlier chapters, the decisions we make about the kinds of people we would like to meet (and marry, for example) and the kinds of people we *actually* meet - who may or may not be the same kind of person - take place within the realities of the population pool. That is to say, it depends on the availability or otherwise of persons of the 'right' age or sex to meet our demands. Again we have also previously observed that there are fewer younger women than men available and, by virtue of a different life expectancy, more available women over the age of 60 (or thereabouts) than men. Population changes *per se* also have an effect on our personal lives when taken in tandem with other dimensions of change, like occupational mobility and marital/divorce trends.

For example for the period 1990-2010, in the case of the UK we will evidence a continuing concentration of population in the south-east of England (excluding Greater London). Northern parts of England - Merseyside, Tyne and Wear, and Lancashire - will continue to suffer significant population losses. Within that period we will also witness a marked drop in those aged between 16 and 21 years of age, while at the same time we will continue to see a steady, unbroken increase in the retired population well into the next century: in fact, *life expectancy* which is greater for female infants than for males, will continue to increase so that by the 2020s a baby boy can expect to live for 76 years and a baby girl for 81 years. At present, life expectancies are about 73 years for a baby boy and 78 for a baby girl (*Social Trends 20:1990 Edition*).

What follows are three examples of possible population changes which could well affect the very fabric of our personal lives:

- *Occupational mobility*, whereby by virtue of particular individuals leaving a region in search of work opportunities, the basic number of available partners may well decrease and another age group, for instance, may have to be turned to.
- Those inclined towards meeting individuals much younger than themselves - for example in the 16 to 21-year-old age bracket - might well have to settle for their own age group, or even older.
- As we live longer we may well have to learn newer ways of making our relationships continue to work or, if we are surviving women, discover other possibilities of creating new relationships or alternatives.

This final example is quite pertinent to our discussion. The simple fact is that as our lifespan has increased over the decades, our ability to sustain relationships has similarly been tested. What was tolerable or bearable in a marriage lasting twenty years, perhaps became less so in one which continued for almost thirty: certainly a clear example of the importance of recognizing that the pattern and shape of relationships is not a static never-changing thing. We, as individuals, both change our lives and institutions *over time*, and in turn are changed by those very same institutions. Through our behaviour we slowly produce new patterns of (say) marriage and divorce and then, subsequently, begin to live in new ways and in keeping with those same 'novel patterns'.

Within the specific realm of marriage and divorce amongst numerous projections as to the uncertain future, are the following quite reasonably based on current and recent trends:

- By the year 2000 only one out of two children will grow up in a 'conventional' family, with parents married when they were born and after they have grown up. Most couples will live together before marrying.

- Since 1980 the number of children born outside marriage has more than doubled. A quarter of all children are born outside marriage and the numbers are set to increase.

- In 1971, 84 per cent of men and 93 per cent of women were married by 30, but by 1987 this dropped to 57 per cent for men and 68 per cent for women.

- Up to a quarter of children will have parents who divorce and many more will have cohabiting parents who split up. If the rate continues, 37 per cent of new marriages are likely to end in divorce, and one in five children before sixteen will see their parents split.

(Family Change, 1990, Family Policy Studies Centre).

The point we are simply making here is that, in fear of over-repetition, *we* do make our own futures and then have to live by them. Or at least we are influenced by them.

If we as individuals, for example, disapprove of divorce yet live in a divorce-ridden culture it may well produce a tension in our behaviour (or our partners'). Again, if it is almost 'normal' to be separated or estranged from our children following divorce, despite the intense pain it creates, *perhaps* we will

149

accept such an outcome more readily than we ought to. And so on.

We have previously, in an earlier chapter, highlighted the bare bones of the changes which have occurred within marriage and divorce over the decades, which amount in essence to a rise in divorce and remarriage *and* divorce-remarriage-divorce-remarriage rates. However, perhaps the following statistic graphically summarizes the degree to which changes occur and futures remain uncertain and, often, are unwelcome:

> ... only about one in eighty of the marriages which were celebrated in 1951 had ended in divorce before the sixth wedding anniversary, whereas over one in nine of the marriages solemnised in 1981 had ended in divorce by the same duration ... (and) ... over one fifth of all the marriages solemnised in 1961, 1966, 1971 and 1976 have already ended in divorce.

> (JOHN HASKEY,
> POPULATION TRENDS, 1988).

AIDS

Our survey members gave the impression that they were all too aware that *love* and *sex* were quite different things, although men appeared a little more prone to the confusion than women. Certainly we all hear at times of women complaining about male infatuation, while men - as we saw earlier - do appear to be *slightly* more interested in the physical characteristics of their partners than do women of men. And we all know men who unceremoniously dump their older women for younger versions - new women invariably chosen not solely for their IQs.

Gore Vidal, famed of course for his cynicism, makes an observation that 'lust and compassion are separate and most people know it' yet, he adds, 'they won't ever face up to it. Instead they insist on putting themselves through all this misery about love'. Perhaps more accurately we may say that the *majority* of people do indeed know the difference between lust and compassion and in their 'permanent' relationships eventually settle for a kind of sensual-intimate relationship somewhat devoid of ecstasy but high on trust and give-and-take.

We actually know very little about the sexual behaviour of the married couple, or indeed the 'permanent' on-going relationship. For most of us such matters are deeply intimate and private, only to be shared in moments of drunken bravado or on the doctor's couch. Besides, most of us are a little fearful of sexuality, despite the assertions we make to the contrary, and thus are somewhat reluctant to talk of it.

Our survey was aimed more at examining the relationship between sexuality and 'love', rather than the pure mechanics of sex itself. What emerged was that however 'good' sex was, it was not enough to form the basis of a fruitful long-term *relationship*. Also we discovered that *overall* 'love' was seen both as different from sex and more important: and that love was very much about those fragile emotions and hard-to-define qualities like 'trust', 'respect', 'companionship', 'warmth', and so on. Some individuals of both genders emphasized, more so than the majority did, a more enthusiastic attitude towards sex, while most saw it as being more directly important with the earlier stages of a relationship than the latter. Some people recognized all too clearly that such a decline in 'ecstatic experience', so to speak, was precisely the reason that some partners (usually men) later searched elsewhere for sexual gratification. Hence the 30 per cent of adultery-led divorce decrees.

As with the difficulties in sustaining a relationship *per se*, achieving sexual contentment or happiness *within* a relationship is similarly a daunting task. Women often have to balance demands from children and partners, tiredness and their biology, with readiness, availability and desire; while men similarly have to engage in balancing all sorts of factors including - for many men - a certain inherited set of *beliefs* as to their sexual rights.

Unfortunately the western culture still produces men who believe that it is predominantly *they* who should obtain most pleasure from sexual intercourse, that it is they who ought to be the dominant partner in sexual relations, and that it is in a sense more permissible (understandable and forgivable) for them to engage in extra-marital sexual affairs, than their partners. We are not saying this is a norm or standard, merely a tendency: witness the widespread sale of (news?) papers which exhibit pictures of partly naked women presented solely as sex objects.

It is also fair to say that there are many women who also would concur and agree that sexual pleasure is a male prerogative. But this is hardly surprising: they are often taught, if not to 'lie back and think of England', certainly that 'when you have kids, you can forget about sex'.

Bertrand Russell, the philosopher and keen observer of the sexual behaviour of men and women, pictured the general situation somewhat bleakly: 'marriage is for women the commonest mode of livelihood, and the total amount of undesired sex endured by women is probably greater in marriage than in prostitution'. But what do we really know of

152

the sexual behaviour of the population, in particular that of the permanently entwined?

Our own survey suggests an average rate of intercourse of about once or twice a week for the permanently involved. Furthermore most partners saw themselves as taking a dominant *and* a subordinate part in the sexual relationship. Most couples agreed that there was, with the passage of time, a waning in the importance of sex within their relationship. All of the couples frowned upon adultery.

Quite recently (1990) Dr Tom Smith of the University of Chicago carried out a major survey into the 'sex lives of the married American', which could prove to be helpful. Amongst his conclusions were that the average American (including the non-married) had sexual intercourse about '57 times' a year and that:

> The American way of sex seems to reflect the traditional mores of a Barbara Cartland novel, unadventurous, fidelity and monogamy...

Dr Smith also reported that almost a quarter of the adult American population will 'go without sex' for an entire year (in any particular year), but that, nonetheless, 'frequency of sexual intercourse was the strongest indicator of how happy a marriage was'. As he himself put it: 'it may be that happy people have sex or that sex makes people happy'.

We concur with the majority of the findings of Dr Smith's survey, although given the high rate of adultery all over the western world (including the USA) he appears a little optimistic over the matter. But clearly it *is* evident that the *majority* of married couples have somewhat unadventurous and predictable sex lives, with sexual activity taking a somewhat minor role in their lives especially as the years pass.

Again, the *future* may well bring changes to the pattern of sexual behaviour; specifically the AIDS epidemic could radically alter our sexual behaviours and expectations. Consider briefly some of the possibilities:

- The fear of AIDS might lead to certain people engaging in sexual activity only with great reluctance and consequently choosing a potential partner more than usually on non-sexual grounds.

- There could well be *less* pre-marital 'living together', with a *possible* consequence being one of more unsatisfactory relationships than at present, and problems surfacing *after* marriage rather than *before* (where they might have surfaced, discussed or been resolved through separation, for example).

- The fear of AIDS could lead to less adulterous behaviour, with 'adulterers' uncertain of the sexual health of their potential partners. One consequence of this could be the rise of more satisfactory marriages with more honesty and energy put into making them work fruitfully, *or* on the other hand the lack of adulterous opportunities could lead ironically to further tension and more marital disharmony.

- Another possibility could be an increase in *celibate* behaviour, with individuals turning away completely from any sexual involvement (either within or, more likely, out of relationships).

154

These are merely a few of the possible consequences of reactions to the AIDS epidemic.

Dr Smith's previously quoted survey observes that a 'significant proportion of the population' are still at 'high risk from their sexual practices'. Our own survey suggested that the majority of couples *were* concerned with the dangers of AIDS and, more than ever, were determined to be monogamous - determined to stick with one partner - while many also talked of using condoms, both for the first time and also for the forseeable future. However there was also evidence of a tiny minority who still believed that AIDS was a disease confined to the gay population and certain drug users.

That there is a divergence of opinion about AIDS is hardly surprising given the fact that it is so recent a development. In spite of its devastating consequences, many people do not want to think about AIDS constructively: especially if they feel that they may have to alter their own sexual behaviour or practices. What actually are the facts?

A recent (1990) WHO (World Health Organization) report talked in terms of there being a total of almost *eight million people* - one in four hundred of the world's adults - who may well be carrying the AIDS virus, HIV. The report concluded that:

> Our current estimate is that by the year 2000 there will be a cumulative total of 15 to 20 million HIV-infected persons worldwide. At least three-quarters of these infections will have occurred in the developing world, and will have resulted from heterosexual transmission.

Of course an HIV infection does not *necessarily* lead to fully blown AIDS; however, the size of the problem is, nonetheless, quite evident. Indeed the recently published government report on 'HIV infection and AIDS in England and Wales', commonly known as the Cox Report, comments that the 'proportion of people infected with HIV who will eventually develop AIDS is uncertain', yet nonetheless concludes that 'some of the recent evidence suggests it is higher than originally thought and may be as high as 80 per cent, or even greater'. In other words, if the WHO predictions turn out to be accurate, we are talking about something like one in every four or five hundred adults in the world having AIDS at the turn of the century - in just a few years' time.

The table shows us, by taking the sole case of England and Wales as examples, that the main cause of AIDS is still by homosexual transmission.

However the conclusions of the report point to a far more *uncertain future*, especially with regard to the potential increase in the transmission of HIV and AIDS through *heterosexual* behaviour. For instance the authors of the Cox Report argue that at the end of 1987 there were 'probably between 20,000 and 50,000 persons infected with HIV in England and Wales, of whom some 13,000 to 30,000 were homosexuals'. However they add that:

> The number infected by heterosexual contact so far is estimated to be between 2,000 and 5,500. However when one adds to this those infected by other means, the number of infected heterosexual adults, which includes most infected drug users and haemophiliac men, is probably around 6,000 to 17,000, so

Transmission categories of reported AIDS cases, cumulative totals, England and Wales, excluding visitors, to 30 June 1988.

Transmission category	Male Cases	(Deaths)	Female Cases	(Deaths)	Total Cases	(Deaths)
Homosexual/bisexual male	1238	(709)			1238	(709)
Injecting drug user (IDU)	17	(12)	3	(2)	20	(14)
Homosexual/bisexual male & IDU	27	(12)			27	(12)
Haemophilliac	99	(61)	1	(1)	100	(62)
Blood/components recipient:						
Abroad	7	(4)	4	(3)	11	(7)
UK	6	(5)	3	(3)	9	(8)
Hetrosexual contact:						
Partner(s) with above risk factors	2	(1)	6	(2)	8	(3)
Others *						
known exposure abroad	21	(4)	8	(6)	29	(10)
no evidence of exposure abroad†	3	(2)	2	(2)	5	(4)
Child of at risk/infected parent	4	(0)	5	(2)	9	(2)
Other/undetermined	12	(6)	1	(1)	13	(7)
Total	1436	(816)	33	(22)	1469	(838)

Notes: * partner(s) not known to have above risk factor(s). † includes persons, without other identified risks, from countries where heterosexual transmission is common

Source: Department of Health, The Welsh Office, London: HMSO

the potential for further heterosexual spread already exists.

The report points out that 'any epidemic in the general heterosexual community, while it would probably grow rather slowly, would ultimately affect very large numbers.'. In a somewhat more optimistic note the authors of the Cox Report add that they have discerned evidence that the numbers of new AIDS cases per month - in England and Wales - while still increasing, are doing so less rapidly, probably 'as a result of behaviour changes in the mid 1980s

Total number of AIDS cases reported in 18 European countries

Country	Mar 86	June86	Sep86	Dec86	Mar87	Jun87	Sep87	Dec87
Austria	34	36	44	54	72	93	120	139
Belgium	160	171	180	207	230	255	277	277
Denmark	80	93	107	131	150	176	202	228
Finland	11	11	14	14	19	19	22	24
France	707	859	1050	1221	1632	1980	2532	3073
W Germany	459	538	675	826	999	1133	1400	1669
Greece	14	22	25	35	42	49	78	88
Ireland	8	9	10	12	14	19	19	25
Israel	23	24	31	34	38	39	43	47
Italy	219	300	367	523	664	870	1104	1411
Netherlands	120	146	180	218	260	308	370	420
Norway	21	24	26	35	45	49	64	70
Portugal	24	28	40	46	54	67	81	90
Spain	145	177	201	264	357	508	624	789
Sweden	50	57	76	90	105	129	143	163
Switzerland	113	138	170	192	227	266	299	355
U.Kingdom	287	340	512	610	729	870	1067	1227
Yugoslavia	3	3	3	8	10	11	21	26

Source: Mariotto (1988)

among the homosexual community.'

This somewhat optimistic observation has to be tempered however by the realization that *heterosexuals*, on the other hand, will presumably *not* change their behaviour until they are actually convinced that AIDS can drasticallay affect *their* lives. So far, although many heterosexuals are 'concerned' about AIDS, many still actually feel 'it couldn't happen to me'.

In conclusion, bearing in mind that we have earlier talked about a post-1992 Europe without frontiers, it may be profitable to look at the European AIDS picture, as shown in the table above in case our ambitions and search for love similarly take on a 'European dimension':

So the pattern and significance of our *future* sexual lives, relationships, marriage and divorce is clearly an *uncertain* one. Population changes, a renaissance of spiritual or religious values, and the spectre of the AIDS epidemic will inevitably create a new shape to our personal lives - which may result in minor or perhaps major changes to the ways in which we live our personal lives.

What *is* certain, however, is that 'love' will continue to act as a magnet for most of us. We will continue to see it as *the* meaning of our lives, of equal or indeed of greater importance than our work lives or careers, or indeed any religious views we may hold. Finding love and a partner, creating a family and growing old in companionship remains the hub of our lives. Why *precisely* should this be so?

Chapter Seven:
The Psychology of Relationships

The problem lay buried, unspoken, for many years in the minds of American women. It was a strange stirring, a sense of dissatisfaction, a yearning that women suffered in the middle of the twentieth century in the United States. Each suburban wife struggled with it alone. As she made the beds, shopped for groceries, matched slip-cover material, ate peanut butter sandwiches with her children, chauffeured Cub Scouts and Brownies, lay beside her husband at night - she was afraid to ask even of herself the silent question - "is this all".

BETTY FRIEDAN.

In a recent survey carried out in Britain (*Woman's Own*, June 26, 1990) a quarter of all women interviewed claimed to have been 'battered' by their men, while one in five of them said they believed their partners had committed adultery, yet nonetheless the majority claimed to be 'content' and indeed 9 out of 10 still hoped to be with 'their man' in 5 years.

In our own survey some women reported that their *previous* partners had been violent on occasions - indeed *that* behaviour was the major reason they had terminated their relationships - while other women had talked of their own violence towards their partner.

160

Some women had hinted at a suspicion of their partners' possible adultery, yet for most of them it was more a fear than a reality. The *majority* of our survey had put past *poor* or failed relationships behind them and started afresh, while the first-timers were still relishing the novelty of it all.

The remarriage rates are enough evidence for us as to the power of 'love'; but if we were in need of further evidence we only have to look at the modern movie, novel, teenage magazine, advertisement, listen to popular music, and so on. From a *very* young age - even before the onset of those adolescent *biological* developments - we are encouraged to embrace the power and importance of love. We have *ideas* about 'love' thrust at us continuously, whether we like it or not. But what exactly is it? Where do such ideas come from? What impact do they have on our lives?

Some psychologists believe that 'love' is similar to a psychotic state, indeed a state of *madness*, while others talk of it in terms of a chemical reaction, with 'love' feelings being seen as similar to amphetamine 'highs', because they believe that the 'loving brain produces its own intoxicating substance, something the doctors call phenylethylamine'. Conversely, the 'spurned brain' goes into a drug withdrawal, 'causing severe craving for chocolate, which itself contains phenylethylamine'.

If we ask any number of people the question 'what is love?', we will inevitably get a set of clichés - togetherness, consideration, kindness, sexual passion, respect, and so on - and equally inevitably we will not be offered many lengthy sentences. This is not surprising: 'love' *is* a difficult term to unpackage, if you like. Our own experiences of 'love' will inevitably be different from others'. Besides, it is constantly and traditionally referred to somewhat mysteriously as something akin to an

161

uninvited-yet-welcome-guest: 'you'll know it when it comes', 'love arrives when you least expect it', and so on.

And, of course, there are those 'conditions' we mistake for 'love', like *infatuation*. For anyone who has experienced it, the condition runs a certain course, like a disease: it invariably has a sudden and violent beginning and an equally sudden end, and is characterized by a sudden dropping of previous ties. The infatuated man or woman can experience 'love' only as long as the love object is reluctant, and consequently lose interest in the partner when love is actually returned.

Another problem in attempting definitions of love is that it takes many different *forms*. The psychoanalyst Martin Bergmann in his *The Anatomy of Loving* lists a number of 'varieties of love' as he calls them, *including* the following:

- ***Triangular love*: many individuals can only love when in a triangle. To psychoanalysts, the ability to love only within a triangle suggests a continued fixation within the Oedipal triangle - when, as a child, a boy 'desired' his mother but knew it to be wrong and therefore feared his father.**

- ***Confidential love*: a situation whereby men and women feel that they can love one person *uniquely* but not *exclusively*. As Bergmann himself explains: 'Many people who fear that loving one person will make them too dependent on the love object or cause them to lose their sense of self find safety in dividing their love between different people. Some know love only as a state of indecision between two or more people. They need not be promiscuous; every one of their loves has its own history and stretches over many years,**

162

but what characterizes every one of these relationships is that they can love only when they love more than one person at a time.'

- *Loveless sexuality*: is the experience of intense sexuality without the accompanying feeling of love.

- *Masochistic love*: Bergmann defines this extremely succinctly: 'Masochistic love is an exaggeration of normal falling in love where everything is sacrificed for the partner; the person lives only through the partner; the partner is magnificent; the person himself or herself is insignificant. For the masochist, falling in love and loving are in the service of suffering. Such people love in order to suffer and to have pain inflicted upon them.'

- *Pygmalion love*: In this form of love we love what we have created. Pygmalion-type lovers need to teach and mould their beloved, showing them the places the other had never visited, books the other had never read, and so on - improving their speech, manners, and the way they dress. Interestingly, according to psychoanalysts such love often, if not always, leads to lasting happy relationships. Pygmalion love becomes endangered when the 'disciple' wishes for equality.

- *Narcissistic love*: In this form of love we love what we are or what we were, or what we wished to have been, or someone who was once part of ourselves.

- *Anaclitic love*: This is the continuation of the love of the child for an adult, the love of the weak for the strong. It is the love of the person who feels inadequate for the person who is (or appears to be) powerful and who has achieved a great deal in life. Often there

**is the wish to be permanently taken care of
and remain dependent on the other.**

There are numerous other examples of such
'varieties of love'. As we have discussed much
earlier, there are also those 'addicts of love' those
'women who love too much' for example, to use
Robin Norwood's terminology. Such addicted
people need love as others need food or drugs.

However when we talk of 'love' we inevitably
think in terms of 'romantic love', of 'falling in love',
of its association with youth. Obviously the capacity
to 'fall in love' when one is old is indeed possible and
does happen. Yet the idea of *romantic love* and its
association with youth is the one that tends *initially*
to colour our definitions and expectations of love and,
moreover, is the one we often use to measure against
the reality of the relationships we find ourselves in.

Romantic love

Romantic love grew most rapidly, if not initially, as
an idea in France during the last quarter of the 12th
century. Its theoretical basis was formulated by
Andreus Capellanus in *The Art of Courtly Love*, and
in the poetry of Chretien de Troyes. Carried through
the countryside by the songs of the troubadours, the
idea of romantic love subsequently took hold and
spread rapidly throughout Europe.

This code of courtly love consisted of the
following elements: the ennobling power of love; the
conception of love as a burning, rarely extinguished
passion; *the impossibility of love between husband
and wife*; the elevation of the beloved to a position
superior to that of the supplicant (in imitation of the
relationship between feudal lord and vassal); and the
idea of fidelity between lovers (at least while they

164

were in love). Other themes dealt with nature, the naturalness of love affairs, the personification of love as a god, and so on.

Importantly this code argued that love thrived on the belief in 'freedom of choice', was spontaneous and, therefore, could not be formalized as, for example, in a marriage 'contract'. As marriage was seen to be a relationship with fixed and specified obligations, *marriage and love* were therefore deemed to be incompatible.

Romanticism was similar to courtly love. The romanticist worshipped that which was natural and that which was unique or idiosyncratic to each person. The romanticist cherished sensation and emotion as essential to life, and was attracted to contrasts, to apposition and antithesis. Above all, the romanticist fuelled his protest with youthful energy: Byron, Shelley, Keats, Wordsworth, Coleridge, Chateaubriand, and Lamartine were all in their twenties or thirties when they made their major contributions to the romantic ideals.

Romantic love is often described as a sweeping, all-encompassing emotion, and often expressed in terms of 'sickness' or sadness - like parting, it is such sweet sorrow. Romantic love is the ideal of pure, unfulfilled love that is celebrated by the poets and acted out in so many of the great dramas - Romeo and Juliet, Tristan and Isolde, Heloise and Abelard being the classic examples.

The importance of physical attraction (and 'beauty'), of extremely strong emotional attachments, the notion of 'love at first sight', the idea that love conquers all; that women are more romantic than men; that there is a predestined one and only love, all these beliefs emerge from the central idea of romantic love.

Critics of the notion of romantic love focus on the fact that romantic love was applicable as an idea *only to love outside of marriage*, yet ironically (since the 16th century, in a sense) this idea has been the very one which has guided us in our marital choice. 'It's no wonder then that so many marriages end in divorce', would be our critics' observation.

Yet as we have earlier indicated, much of contemporary popular culture - the music industry, movies, teenage magazines - celebrates this ideal of romantic love, while indeed many of us continue to believe in it or at least some part of it.

Interestingly, there are also a few defenders of the idea within psychology, perhaps most notably Ethel Person in her best-selling book *Love and Fateful Encounters*. In this book she rejects the usual *realistic* or *rational* definition of love as 'physical gratification with a happy relationship' because, she believes, our actual experiences of passionate love belies such an oversimplified definition. Such a definition ignores, she claims, 'love's magnetic pull, its peremptoriness and imaginative power'. In a nutshell, her central theme is that:

> ... love serves an important function not only for the individual but also for the culture. It is the narrative thread not just in novels, but in lives. Love determines one's sense of obligations and time, or transforms them. Romantic love offers not just the excitement of the moment but the possibility for dramatic change in the self. It is, in fact, an agent of change.

She believes that *overall* romantic love is more 'enriching than it is depleting', and that despite its often transient nature it 'offers access to the

166

unconscious, lights up the emotional life, and brings internal change in a way that often far outlives the experience itself'. She interestingly concludes that romantic love:

> ... is the preserve of hope and imaginative longing; it is one of the passions that move us, that initiate the great quests and adventures of our lives. Like so many other human gifts, romantic love has the potential for both good and evil, but should not be judged by its corrupted forms or dismissed on account of its transience.

More specifically what she is arguing is not merely the cliché - 'it is better to have loved and lost, than never to have loved at all' - but rather that romantic love is an experience that genuinely, *psychologically speaking*, might enrich any relationships that follow. For example: not often, but occasionally, the intensity and passion of the initial phase of romantic love may persist and find a place within a committed, sustained love. She additionally speaks of the learning opportunities inherent in romantic love: for example, in love we are attempting to be loved for what we are; yet at the very same time we are seeking an escape to a newer, broader, co-operative *self*. And so on.

One of the most perceptive critics of the influence that 'romantic love' has had on our personal lives is Erich Fromm who, in his *The Art of Loving*, posed the question: 'Is love an art?' If it actually is, he asserts, it requires knowledge and effort. Or is love a pleasant sensation experienced by chance, something one 'falls into' if one is lucky? Fromm believes the former while he considers that the majority of people believe in the latter. In particular he sees three sets of problems. First, most people see the problem of love primarily as that of being loved rather than that of loving, of one's capacity to love. Second, is the related assumption that the problem of love is the problem of an object, not the problem of a faculty. Most people, Fromm considers, think that to love is simple, but that to find the right object to love, or to be loved by is difficult. He persuasively argues (as we have also discussed previously) that western culture is itself based on the appetite for buying, on the idea of a mutually favourable exchange and so we may well look at people in a similar way: 'For the man an attractive girl - and for the woman an attractive man - are the prizes they are after. "Attractive" usually means a nice package of qualities which are popular and sought after on the personality market.' Two persons thus 'fall in love' when they feel they have found the best object available on the market, considering the limitations of their own exchange values.

The third error, Fromm believes, lies in the confusion between the initial experience of 'falling' in love, and the permanent state of being in love, or as we might better say, of 'standing' in love. Fromm argues that this 'miracle' of sudden intimacy is often facilitated if it is combined with, or initiated by, sexual attraction and consummation. However, this type of love is by its very nature not lasting. The two persons become well acquainted, their intimacy loses more and more its miraculous character, until their antagonism, their disappointments, their mutual boredom kill off whatever is left of the initial excitement.

Love is ...

Much of what Fromm argues is supported by the findings of our survey: that physical attraction is *not* that important, that love needs working at in order to sustain it, that love is something to do with trust,

168

respect, give-and-take, and faithfulness. It is, however, also important to remember that many of our couples were well into their second (or third) important relationships and had learned lessons from their previous relationships, and indeed had 'chosen' their new partner on that basis.

So the question is, if the committed, mature, sustaining love which fuels long-term relationships is different to romantic love how best can we describe it and what precisely is its function?

To begin with there are elements of romantic love which remain in 'committed mature love', as we may term it. Not perhaps the ecstasy or the excitement, but rather the desire - partially expressed in romantic love, fully (and genuinely) expressed in mature love - *to become one with another*. It seems to us difficult to improve on this description, offered while nonetheless bearing in mind that *at the same time* the mature lovers also desire to be independent in some areas of their lives (and relationships). Perhaps it is easier to attempt an understanding of love's function than a description of it - perhaps in an important sense love *is* beyond words.

When we talk of love's function we are *not* talking about such things as the delights of companionship and of sharing - of pursuing similar interests, of giving each other support and comfort at moments and times of crisis. Rather we are more interested in the *root* function of love: a love so strong that we may kill to possess it, something so needed, so important, that it becomes the central defining point of our lives. The psychoanalyst Martin Bergmann argues, quite correctly in our opinion, that our need to love (and be loved) is due to our

> ... prolonged helplessness as an infant and equally due to the great

169

intellectual development that takes place during this early period. It seems beyond dispute that after a few months when the baby responds to any caretaker, the baby is happy in the presence of the person or persons that take care of him and sad and miserable when they are away. Under normal conditions, the capacity to enjoy and be happy in the presence of the main caretakers is an inherent capacity in the human being equivalent to the capacity to walk and speak. Out of the alternation between the presence and absence of the caretaking person the emotion of longing emerges.

Loving replaces longing. Indeed one of the main characteristics of the state of being in love consists in the beloved being psychically present and emotionally available at all times even when the beloved is not physically present.

Not surprisingly, such a view sees another major function of love, other than just that of re-finding, namely an attempt to make up for what was missed in childhood, to make up for the many shortcomings and cruelties which parents inadvertently or sometimes sadistically inflicted upon the child. As Bergmann himself puts it, 'consciously or unconsciously we all ask that the love partner be also the healer of our earlier wounds'. A daunting task indeed.

Of course immediately the dilemma is obvious: on the one hand we wish to *re-find* the love object we loved in our childhood, yet on the other we also wish to find a person who will heal wounds received in that very same childhood. Certainly much unhappiness with our loved one (love can be so painful), is due to this same *conflict* between the wish to '*re-find* the old' and the wish to have a love object very different from the old. If a good balance between these contradictory wishes (often unconsciously desired) can be found, Bergmann adds, 'happy love becomes possible'.

Choosing Partners

Clearly at the most profound level we can *never* know precisely why two people find their relationship together fulfilling and compatible. Much of what goes on psychologically at the initial stage of attraction and within the later on-going relationship is operated at both sub- and unconscious levels. What precisely our psychological needs consist of are often unknown to us ourselves let alone others, including our partners. Indeed relationships are in a real sense journeys of such self-discovery in relationship with another interested party.

In other words the *core* of mate selection is somewhat of a mystery - that particular one per cent of uncertainty, which some would term a magical ingredient. Having said that, it is also clear that relationships also have less profound functions than re-finding and healing. Often such relationships function simply to remove boredom and inertia from our lives (though the unsuccessful ones may well, of course, be the actual *cause* of such inertia). To pass the time. To find a reasonably compatible sexual partner. And so on.

Social psychologists have spent a great number of years attempting to understand the processes involved in mate selection, and have *tended* to conclude that relationships are based on *similarity, not complementarity*. In other words, dominant people do, they argue, tend to select dominant partners, just as submissive people choose other submissive people. As we shall later argue this does not appear to us to be particularly accurate, and we will offer an alternative proposition.

At the risk of stating the obvious, data show that couples tend to resemble each other in qualities such as attractiveness, 'personality', IQ, education, socioeconomic class, politics, religion, and social attitudes generally - according to the psychologists. And such psychologists have agreed that such couples tend even to look alike - with similar faces and bodies. This tendency, they argue, is evident even in the early stages of the relationship not just later on, following years of similar patterns of behaviour or habits.

Much of the aforementioned is true, if somewhat superficial. *Our* couples for example *tended* to choose on the basis of *similar interests and values*, however, we gained the impression of a *partial* desire for a *complementarity* of personality traits. Nothing too extreme, nothing *too* different, merely complementary emphases of significance, even if not spectacularly so. In a sense if love is - as we have argued - concerned with becoming part of a whole, with someone else, of completion, of extending ourselves, then *inevitably* our partners will have certain important qualities we ourselves do not possess.

It is the ability to fruitfully sustain relationships *over time* that is the true measure. Are these long-term relationships, these marriages, the true embodiment of our search for love? Our search for completion? The end of longing? For Helge Rubenstein, editor of The Oxford Book of Marriage, the answer is certainly 'yes':

> ... marriage becomes a crucible for
> psychological growth, allowing the
> individual to break through inhibi-

tions and self-imposed limitations, and provides the most nurturing, healing and fulfilling area of a person's life.

In terms of making relationships work, *our* couples have highlighted elements such as sexual compatibility, mutual respect, give-and-take, positive communication, faithfulness, honesty, and shared interests. For them marriage is about happiness *and* compassion, the heat of passion and the craving for identity. None of them pretended that such relationships were easy: indeed many had previously been involved in failed partnerships. Anthony Clare, the psychiatrist, in a most perceptive contribution to the debate, describes the 'normal' life of successful relationships. For most of us, he argues, marriage means expectations and they in turn mean 'conflict'.

> Most modern marriages involve partners who start out sharing a great deal in common, particularly social class, religious background and educational attainment. Both parties bring to that marriage substantial expectations, and the development of more limited, realistic expectations often becomes a key factor in determining whether a marriage survives. Before people can develop such realism, however, they seem to have to negotiate a period of trying to change or alter the spouse so that he or she can somehow fulfil and gratify them.

This period of change or conflict that Clare refers to, adds up to a 'classic pattern' revolving around issues of power, nurture, intimacy, trust and communication:

- *Power:* one or other spouse actively tries to control the relationship, or, more commonly, each spouse is actually afraid of being controlled. Unresolvable problems arise from a poor selection of a partner - for example, when two dominant individuals marry (social psychologists please note).

- *Nurture:* If power is about controlling, nurture is all about caring. A successful marriage has to be one in which both partners are willing and able to care for each other.

- *Intimacy*: an ability to be emotionally close to one another. A *balance* of *needs* works best.

- *Trust*: Here our partner has our interests at heart and will *not knowingly* wound. Contemporary marriage strongly emphasizes trust, which it often equates with fidelity.

- *Communication*: We tend to help each other if we communicate a *little,* but *often.*

Power, nurture, intimacy, trust, communication - these are the demands, the ideals, the expectations which constitute the bones and muscles of the marital relationship, to which of course could be added such things as self-sacrifice, salvation and meaning. Adding up to love.

We could do no better than conclude this discussion on the meaning and psychology of relationships than repeat Clare's own conclusion:

> Rightly or foolishly, we seek through a long-term commitment to, and intimate association with, another person a greater awareness of who or what we are, have been and can become, we learn what we can take and what can break us,

174

develop or lose our sense of worth, esteem and self-regard.

Chapter Eight:
Choosing Partners

A 52-year-old man had been in close contact with his physician during his wife's terminal illness with lung cancer. Examination, including electrocardiogram, 6 months before her death, showed no evidence of coronary disease. He died suddenly of a massive myocardial infarction the day after his wife's funeral.

A 40-year-old father slumped dead as he cushioned the head of his son lying injured in the street beside his motorcycle.

A 17-year-old boy collapsed and died at 6 a.m., June 4, 1970; his older brother had died at 5.12 a.m., June 4, 1969, of multiple injuries incurred in an auto accident several hours earlier. The cause of the younger boy's death was massive sub-arachnoid haemorrhage caused by a ruptured anterior communicating artery aneurysm.

A 55-year-old man died when he met his 88-year-old father after a 20-year separation; the father then dropped dead.

JAMES LYNCH

American researcher James Lynch believes that the lack of human companionship, the sudden loss of love, and chronic human loneliness are significant contributors to serious disease and premature death. His research, reported in *The Broken Heart: The Medical Consequences of Loneliness*, distinguishes between those factors which *predispose* us to conditions such as cardiovascular disease, and factors which *precipitate* immediate heart changes, some of which can lead to sudden death. The examples above are just a few of the many Lynch provides of sudden deaths caused by 'emotional factors'.

However it is not just bereavement that can cause so much harm. For example, Lynch proceeds to argue, on the basis of mortality statistics, that for all ages, for both sexes, and for all races in the USA, the non-married have higher death rates, sometimes as much as five times higher than those of married individuals. He specifically concentrates on the disruption of human relationships that has occurred in the USA as a result of the rapidly increasing divorce rate, and subsequent cases of loneliness. Lynch then concludes that 'people desperately need each other, that we really are dependent on each other.' In the following chapter we will look more closely at whether we do indeed 'desperately *need* each other'; however at this juncture we may agree with Lynch that feelings of *loneliness* do certainly exist and moreover most of us are involved in a search for a partner in order to avoid such feelings.

Loneliness

The world of fiction has, of course, for many years explored loneliness as a central predicament of human drama. Defoe's *Robinson Crusoe*, George Eliot's *Silas Marner*, Bronte's *Wuthering Heights*,

Hesse's *Steppenwolf*, Thomas Wolfe's *Look Homeward Angel* and Hemingway's *The Old Man and the Sea* are but a few examples. Suzanne Gordon in her sociological and most moving study *Lonely in America* argues, however, that loneliness, once a philosophical problem, 'spoken of mainly by poets and prophets, has now become an almost permanent condition for millions of Americans', and that 'knowing no limits of class, race, or age, loneliness today is a great leveller, a new American tradition'. It is a human emotion 'common to all people in all eras', but at certain points in history, through specific social changes, what were 'inevitable moments in life' become, sometimes overnight, lifestyles for millions of people - changes such as increased geographical mobility, the death of a loved one and divorce on an unprecedented scale. So what precisely *is* loneliness? How may we describe or characterize it?

Gordon suggests that loneliness seems to 'universally indicate the following major components': feelings of hopelessness, which lead people to escape into relationships that may appear solidly, grounded but are really only a means to another end, not an end in itself; fear of actually experiencing such feelings of loneliness; the desire to deny that we are in fact lonely; and feelings of worthlessness and failure because of our experience of loneliness.

Quite obviously the desire for company is the major characteristic of loneliness. Indeed the responsiveness of loneliness to the right sort of relationship is quite remarkable - given the establishment of such a relationship, - 'loneliness' will vanish abruptly and without trace, as though it had never existed. There is no gradual recovery, no getting over it bit by bit: when it ends, it ends suddenly - once we were lonely, now we are not.

Loneliness is not depression. In depression we surrender utterly to our distress, while in loneliness we try to rid ourselves of distress by initiating a new relationship or regaining a lost one. The lonely, in other words, have the urge to find others, and if these are believed to be the 'right' ones, they change and we no longer feel lonely. The depressed, however, are often unwilling to impose their unhappiness on others, and their feelings are in any case often unaffected by relationships, old or new.

Our feelings, thought and sensations, when lonely, vary not only from individual to individual, but also in strength. We may look pale, dejeted and hopeless. We may have physical sensations of sickness and cold. We feel sad, uncertain, misunderstood, frightened and aimless. We miss having people around us with whom we can share both joy or sorrow. We feel inner emptiness and a conviction that there is no cure to this hopeless situation unless we quickly find a mate. We accept that people are by nature unwilling to rescue us from our loneliness, that we are left to our own fate.

In the USA, to take but one example, there are over 16 million persons living alone - equivalent to over 21 per cent of all American households - wether as a consequence of deliberate choice, divorce or death. In Britain the statistics of widowhood similarly are quite overwhelming. One woman in seven, and one woman in two over the age of 65, is a widow; and daily 500 wives become widows. But none of these people are necessarily lonely. Indeed for a great number of people being alone, living in a state of solitude is both a desired and welcome state: a point we will return to in our final chapter.

Given the fact that most of us desire a partner to love, cherish and build a long-term fruitful relationship with, how do we go about it? In earlier chapters we looked at how our specifications as to

179

what would constitute our 'ideal partner' may well not be realistic. Quite simply there may not, for example, be enough tall, blonde, fat, dark, Catholic - or whatever - individuals available. And that may well be the case even if we lower expectations and more realistically simply attempt to meet someone just like 'ourselves'.

There are numerous changes in the population which might reduce the number of potential partners, while we might have to move around the country because of our occupations, and so on. And of course, *most* significantly, once *we* have found *our* perfect partner, we have then to convince *them* that they have found *theirs*.

Traditionally in western cultures such a situation has merely been viewed as either natural or simply one of the trials of 'growing up'. We ourselves, even in our darkest moments of resignation, always seem to feel that we will one day meet that special person; that before too long our dreams or prayers will be answered - often mysteriously so, as if by magic.

Usually that is precisely what happens, which in itself is hardly surprising given the amount of time and effort we put into our search for a mate. 'Do teenagers think about anything else?', we may well ask ourselves. Not that it applies simply to them.

In the main most of us meet our loved ones through our places of work or in our social lives. A chance meeting leads to eventual permanence, or a blind date turns out as a pleasant surprise. Sometimes we 'fall in love' quickly and with one of the first people we meet, while others of us spend years refining our own particular requirements. On the other hand some of us are spectacularly poor at the dating game, and fail repeatedly and miserably. However, as we have said, most of us believe this to be the way it is, the natural history of the search for love and companionship.

Other cultures and other traditions, and other historical periods, have produced alternative ways of meeting. Instead of leaving it to *chance* such cultures and traditions have arranged liaisons and marriages. Indeed in our own western cultures particular classes, ethnic groups and religions still to this day engage in such practices. The British aristocracy, for instance, is loathe to allow their members to marry just anyone and prefer to encourage their members to be circumspect and exclusive in their mate selection. This is not to say that they positively debar certain liaisons, rather there is encouragement through the channels of social arrangements of like - meeting - like.

Similarly numerous Asian groupings in Britain continue to practise a form of arranged marriage or, more properly speaking, the semi arranged marriage. With such an arrangement, parents - often in tandem with a professional, commercial marriage bureaux - encourage their children to meet (and marry) an individual from a particular chosen family. However the final decision as to whether to marry or not is invariably left with the said children (the young adults). Within certain Jewish traditions the matchmaker continues to ply his trade, the rabbi often taking on such a role, and in other cultures overseas this tradition of a third party arranging liaisons and marriages is quite widespread.

The belief held by such traditions is that the arranged or semi arranged marriage is preferable to that of *chance* essentially because of four reasons:

- The arranged marriage quite simply *does* solve a person's problems in that a partner will inevtiably be found for them.

- The arranged marriage both helps protect and continue traditional life and, for instance, prevents the young from falling prey to such notions as 'romantic love.'

- The arranged marriage is based on the realistic and honourable expectation of the marriage of family-to-family rather than the more fragile one of individual-to-individual.
- The arranged marriage recognizes and respects the fact that parents actually *do* know best, or at least have years of experience and knowledge on which to base their thoughts on the course that 'love' invariably takes, and the best foundations for fruitful marriages.

Quite simply, at times - in numerous cultures, past and present - it is only through the arranged marriage that people meet *at all*. Accidents of geography, changing traditions, personal psychological inabilities, and so on, are all features which may render an individual's chances on the marriage market somewhat obsolete. For such people, *chance* meetings never seem to happen.

However even today the issue is far from a simple one as for instance Peter Cannon explains through an example from the distant orient:

> Japan has a problem. Japanese girls don't want to marry Japanese farmers any more and by the end of the century over half the villages in Japan could be ghost towns. In the postwar economic bonanza young men and women poured into the cities, turning their backs on the countryside and their parents' feudal traditions. But the eldest sons in Japanese farming families have missed out, bound by tradition to look after ageing parents, inherit the farm, produce an heir and carry on

the bloodline. Today, Japanese girls ... don't want the same lives as their mothers "down on the farm", living with their husbands' parents, so they have packed up and left. In some villages the ratio of farmer bachelors to single girls is as high as 40 to one.

In rural Japan *omy-ai*, arranged marriages, are the tradition, and finding a suitable partner was the responsibility of matchmakers - usually parents or relatives. Protecting property and the family bloodline was always the main criterion. But the rapid migration of young women has made this system obsolete. The lack of young women is so acute that it has ceased to be merely a personal problem - it has become a question of survival for whole communities.

Some villages have organized street demonstrations and, earlier this year, farmers from Akita looking for love and marriage drove their tractors through Tokyo's Shibuya fashion district, handing out leaflets and "Meet a Farmer" disco-party invitations to every OL (Office Lady) and single girl they could see. Sadly for them, there were few takers.

Within our Western cultures, commercial enterprises function to solve the problems of finding a suitable mate for the many of us who will find ourselves at such a loss. Perhaps it is almost unneccesary to repeat the self-evident observation that such a situation is neither grossly unlikely nor anything to be ashamed of. Certainly as we have earlier hinted, the AIDS epidemic to name but one uncertain aspect of the future, will invariably make the marital market an even more unpredictable and hazardous course than it already is.

The contemporary 'introduction industry' functions in a similar manner to that of the traditional matchmaker although commercial gain is the prime motivating force. This is not to be critical, simply to state the obvious difference between the two. The industry itself can be categorized in the following manner, according to differences in both the major functions and techniques, although many agencies have more than one major function and similarly employ a combination of techniques:

- Marriage Bureaux: The function is obviously to help persons marry rather than simply to 'date'. The techniques used involve questionnaires, together with personal interviews.

- Computer Dating: The function here primarily is of introducing people initially for dates and usually, but not necessarily, marriage. The technique uses a questionnaire, with the data supplied being then processed by a computer.

- Introduction and dating agencies: These agencies function to introduce people for dates, friendship or marriage, and use questionnaires and on occasions, interviews.

- The list technique: On the basis of information derived from questionnaires these agencies provide members with lists of other members containing personal details and sometimes even photographs. It is then the perogative of members to contact one another for a possible date. The eventual outcome may be a long-term friendship or even marriage.

184

- Video dating: These agencies record agency members in an interview situation, and subsequently other members view the video and choose their date. A desire for long term relationships is the norm here.

- Specialist agencies: These agencies, which range from marriage bureaux to dating organizations, are characterized by a concentration on particular 'client groups', *eg* Asians or gays, etc.

There are other types of agencies which do not neatly fall into the aforementioned categories, while the 'personal ads' industry is also sometimes lumped together with them.

The introduction agency has its fierce critics: it is believed by many that the proprietors of such agencies exploit the lonely for commercial gain. The reality is somewhat different. There are undoubtedly some agencies which, by virtue of either naive management or ruthlessness, do not function particularly efficiently or compassionately. *Some* are quite immoral. However the majority of the members of the industry function and behave properly; operating within a most , problematic area of human life they indeed have a thankless task. Even the most efficient and well - run agencies face two extremely challenging problems: first, that we, as potential clients, are invariably a little bit unrealistic as to our expectations in terms of what kind of person we would like to meet and what kind of person we believe would be attracted to us; and second the problem of the lack of available agency members - both in number and types of individuals. An agency may well have a great number of 'available' widows over 55 years of age on its books, but does it also have a sufficient number of men over 60? Does it have any women under the age of 25? Are they all living nearby? And so on.

Despite its inherent uncertainty the future will, it seems to us, expand the number of agencies operating within the introduction industry as demand itself increases. People will inevitably find the marriage maket more complex, and difficult to manage. They will turn to computer dating, to marriage bureaux, in search of a solution. Because they will have been warned about such agencies, many will feel stigmatized, guilty. However there is a positive side too.

There is absoutely nothing to be ashamed of in turning for help in a search for a partner. In itself the search is difficult enough; if additionally we are not well blessed with social and communicative skills, or are simply unlucky, the task becomes even more daunting. As well as possibly finding a partner for us, the agency we turn to may also be able to achieve two other things. By virtue of the inevitable 'screening' procedures that well- run agencies operate, undesirable individuals are banished - and with the alarming growth in sexual and violent crimes, such security is welcome and valued. Second when we turn to an agency we *inevitably* have to focus our minds on the kind of person we think we would like to meet - indeed the kind of person we think we *want*; what kinds of qualities we are looking for in a potential life long partner; what kind of person we believe we are, and the sort of qualities we believe we possess. Too many people only think about such things following failed relationships; perhaps a previous amount of forethought might have prevented undue misery or pain.

Conclusions:
In Search of Love

We sense that there can be no true communion
between human beings until they have in fact become
beings: for to be able to give oneself one must have
taken possession of oneself in that painful solitude
outside of which nothing belongs to us and we have
nothing to give ...   LOUIS LAVELLE

Spare a thought for those who feel unable to love or
are destined to live alone, without long-term love.
They are the people who *are* lonely. Yet there are
those who choose to remain unloved and live alone
and are happy with such a state of affairs. The
following three accounts are offered by lonely people,
'ordinary people', unable to either find or keep love
in their lives. First 'John', aged 36:

**'After having counselling and reading a lot of
books, I now feel I'm unable to commit myself to
anyone as if I feel drawn to a lady for closeness,
then when things get deeper I always find a way
out ...'**

'Sam', aged 29:

**'I meet lots of nice girls at work...and I can hold
fairly good conversations with them. Some of them
I'd like to be an "issue" with, to be important to
them, but I won't do anything about it because I
don't know what to do that is any different from
what I've done before that has ended in failure and
unhappiness, and so I tell myself I'm not really**

interested after all. But I want to be loved and feel the need to be held.'

And 'Margaret', aged 43:

... none of my relationships have really worked out, ever. Since the age of 18 I've been out with about thirty people, of which perhaps half a dozen were special relationships; the rest were companions and/or lovers. Apart from an unrealistic "first love" at the age of 16, I have fallen in love only twice - neither person was in love with me; although both very very fond of me. Only one person has ever fallen in love with me - I was not in love with him ... I *do* seem to lack that vital spark which keeps people loving me - perhaps I am not very loveable. I think I am also destructive in relationships, although I can be loving and affectionate, thoughtful, and sexual, and once I love someone (whether "in love" or not), I do not stop loving them at all easily ... And, yes, I did feel unloved by my parents especially as a teenager and young adult ...

Perhaps 'Margaret' is trying too hard to fill the longing need she has to be loved - doubtless the result of being unloved by her parents in the past. Perhaps her efforts overwhelm those she becomes involved with. However it is extremely difficult to understand precisely both the causes of these loveless lives and find solutions for them. Solutions - if a love object is not to be secured - vary, although many focus on the 'improvement' of an individual's social and communicative skills. Even then many of us still fail to make contact.

Loving Oneself

There is another alternative, namely the desire and ability to be *alone*. This faculty, can be a particularly strong and positive one, or it can develop out of a sense of resignation.

Paradoxically, this 'ability to be alone', a much ignored faculty in our somewhat couple-obsessed culture, might not only cushion us from the disappointments of not being in love with another, but additionally it could develop those aspects of our personality which *ultimately enable us to engage in mature, long-term relationships*.

We are certainly *not* pretending that the development or sustenance of such an ability is in any way easy. Solitude can drive us inwards, demand that we face our particular problems, ensure there is no escape, and force us to rely on ourselves - no shoulder to cry on - very painful!

Anthony Storr, a practising psychotherapist, points out that both for him and for many other therapists, the criterion of emotional maturity is the 'capacity of the individual to make mature relationships on equal terms', and adds that the 'capacity to be alone' is also an aspect of such emotional maturity. He refers favourably to a classic paper by the late British psychoanlayst Donald Winnicott, '*The capacity to be alone*', where the author wrote:

It is probably true to say that in psycho analytical literature more has been written on the *fear* of being alone or the *wish* to be alone than on the *ability* to be alone ... [and] ... it would seem to me that a discussion on the positive aspects of the capacity to be alone is overdue.

Storr, for one, has taken up such a challenge. He argues that 'love and friendship are, of course, an important part of what makes life worthwhile' but, he adds, they are 'not the only source of happiness.' Moreover, Storr continues, human beings change and develop as life goes on: in old age 'human relationships often become less important.'

189

Interestingly, Storr points to the inherent element of uncertainty in our interpersonal relationships which should, he believes, preclude us from seeing them as the absolute or only path towards personal fulfilment. Indeed, he continues, if we 'did not look at marriage as the principal source of happiness, fewer marriages would end in tears.' So what precisely does Storr point to as being a 'source of happiness', in addition to that of love and friendship?

> I shall argue that interests, whether in writing history, breeding carrier pigeons, speculating in stocks and shares, designing aircraft, playing the piano, or gardening, play a greater part in the economy of human happiness than modern psycho-analysts and their followers allow ... [and] ... we must all have known people whose lives were actually made worthwhile by such interests, whether or not their human relationships were satisfactory. The burden of value with which we are at present loading interpersonal relationships is too heavy for these fragile craft to carry. Our expectation that satisfying intimate relationships should, ideally provide happiness and that, if they do not, there must be something wrong with those relationships, seems to be exaggerated.

So Storr emphasizes the importance of 'interests' as a sustaining force in our lives: as an element of considerable importance, on a par with love and friendship.

We perhaps suspect a little difference in the opinions of the two sexes here: it seems to us that the possibility which Storr has described is more likely to be embraced by men than women. Whether by virtue of conditioning *or* some sort of innate proclivity women *do* appear a little more interested in the importance of interpersonal relationships. Besides, men tend to have more free time to develop interest in hobbies, etc. What however *is* certain that over recent decades - fuelled essentially by the persuasive arguments of feminism - many of us have attempted to reshape some of the contours of our relationships. While some of us have been happy to 'let things be as they *were*' in our parents' time, many more of us have been forced into a rethink. This is a worldwide phenomenon.

In a provocative book titled *Love in America: Gender and Self Development*, Francesca Cancian assesses the claim that the self-centredness of individuals developed in some cultures over the recent decades has strained to breaking point marriage and the family. After surveying what she considers to be the evidence, she does *not* agree with the claim that the bonds of reciprocity and enduring commitments which are necessary for marriage and the family fundamentally conflict with self-development. Rather she believes in a third possibility, a 'new image of love that combines enduring love with self-development', which indeed has already emerged: 'many Americans believe that to develop their individual potential, they need a supportive, intimate relationship with their spouse or lover', and moreover that these people see self-development and love as mutually reinforcing, not conflicting. In this image, love and self-development grow from the mutual *interdependence* of two people, not from extreme independence, not from the one-way dependency of a woman on a man as encouraged by traditional marriage.

191

	Who is responsible for love?	What is love?
Feminized love Family Duty (19th century)	Woman	Fulfil duty to Family
Companionship (1920 -)	Woman	Intimacy in marriage
Androgynous love Independence	Woman and Man	Individual self-development and intimacy
Interdependence (1970 -)	Woman and Man	Mutual self-development, intimacy and support

Source: Cancian (1987)

Cancian talks of more flexible gender roles, and increasing concern with private life and the expression of feelings. Americans, she observes, increasingly describe a good marriage or love relationship in terms of both 'partners communicating openly, developing an autonomous self, and working on the relationship.' In this apparently new and complex 'idea of love' the man and woman are *equally responsible* for the relationship, both openly 'dependent on the other', and yet committed to self-development.

Cancian schematically chronicles the major changes, as she sees them in the table above:

There are people, however, who can see little, if any, evidence of changing gender roles, with couples almost Neanderthaly carrying on traditions demanding dependence and subordination. There is *talk* though. For example in Britain there is the talk of an impending New Age of consciousness and spirituality, and with it comes the idea of the new man. This subject has been examined only superficially and as yet very little hard evidence can be brought to bear on it. Interestingly enough, however, a recent survey carried out by a multinational advertising agency, 'Grey's', into the reality (or otherwise) of the so-called 'new man', concluded that after '30 years of female liberation', half of the male population hasn't made even the 'slightest effort to change'. In the survey one in four men believed that a woman's place was 'in the home', while one in three believed that *he* should be 'the breadwinner'.

But probably the idea of a pervasive 'chauvinistic man' is really just as much a fallacy as the rise of the 'new man'. Most men for a long time, it seems to us, have been caught in a 'transition', caught in the middle ground between the two extremes: no longer do they wish to be dinosaurs, but neither are they quite ready to become, as they see it, completely emasculated.

Compromising Love

Not all men are rapists, as a few misguided people would have it, neither are they all afraid of intimacy. There are also some women who, just like men, are confused, lost, messed up, and quite as capable of cruelty toward a partner as men are. Not that men and women automatically behave the same way in

193

relationships. There does seem to be a tendency in men to substitute authority for affection in their relationships with their children, and they do tend to seek mother substitutes in their wives to an alarming degree, while searching for father substitutes in the workplace.

In a comment meant to be damning of the male psyche, Heather Formani, argues that:

> A man often reverts to the time-hon-
> oured system of marrying a woman
> he doesn't quite love, and loving a
> woman he cannot marry. In this
> way he can maintain a state of ideal-
> ism about love and yet never face
> the reality of it.

But does this apply just to men? We might well ask. For many of us - both men and women - realize that the combination of 'marriage and love' is not necessarily an ideal one; that it may well be something of a compromise; feel that 'love' should be somehow more exciting, more profound, *less* like a cosy, warm and comfortable set of clothes. Many of us settle for a partner who does *not* possess *all* of the qualities we were searching for, without that 'vital spark' that sets them apart from other humans. Another compromise.

That our relationships and marriages are often not perfect is evident from the surveys which report an alarming rise in the rate of *adultery*. One survey argues that it is indeed *increasingly* women, not men, who are the first to stray from their relationships, and moreover claims that almost half of them take at least one lover during any one given marriage. The same survey adds that in the case of men, almost 65 per cent of married men stray by the age of 40. The survey concludes by talking of the 'shrinking fidelity plan': British women who married before 1960 lasted 14 years and men 11 years before embarking on an affair, whereas currently the comparative figures suggest that women wait 4 years, men 5, before being unfaithful.

Yet we persevere in our search for love - in a sense there is little choice. We have a longing, a void that needs to be satisfied. *Learning to love ourselves* - or at least developing the capacity to be alone - may well help us from allowing ourselves to be overwhelmed in unproductive relationships.

Social psychologists in discussing aspects of long-term on-going relationships have tended to agree on a number of things, including the following:

- On *average*, 'mutual regard' fades as a marriage gets longer.
- The so-called 'honeymoon period' lasts for about 3 to 4 years.
- Those who marry young are *more likely* to divorce.
- It is generally found that the arrival of children causes a deterioration in the quality of the relationship.
- On the whole, the higher the income the more satisfactory the marriage.
- In general the more 'educated' have better marital relationships than the less educated. On the other hand, it also seems important that partners are similar in this respect, and particularly important that the woman is not more highly qualified than the man.
- Religious people tend to have more satisfying marriages.
- Remarriage is fairly common among divorcees; remarriages are generally more likely to end in divorce than are first marriages;

remarriages also end in divorce more quickly than do first marriages.

- It can be argued that emotionally healthy parents produce children with good family relations.

- An individual's *private* feelings contribute positively to a relationship and what outsiders think is largely irrelevant. If anything, other people finding their partner attractive is a drawback.

- A good relationship is good for you but it is better to have no relationship at all than it is to have a bad one.

And, in conclusion, such social psychologists believe that the following things are all interconnected:

considering the relationship successful, not wanting to terminate it, feeling fortunate to be with that particular person, claiming to be happy, to love them and to feel loved by them, to respect them and to feel respected by them, to be proud of them and to feel that they are proud of you, wanting to be with them, enjoying your time with them, feeling that you understand them and they understand you, trusting them, wanting to touch and cuddle them, feeling attracted to them, thinking that they are attracted to you, enjoying sex with them, not experiencing conflicting feelings about them, not being irritated by them, feeling there is a romantic side to the relationship, that there is enough give and take, enough kindness, and considering companionship to be important.

It is an understatement to say that people who feel this way towards someone who in turn reciprocates the feelings are fortunate. Many of *our* couples were indeed fortunate - many of them because of the learning gained from previous failed relationships. All were involved in the search for love; some believed they had now found it.

How can we conclude? A possible summary could be that we expect too much from marriage (and other long-term relationships), and too little from ourselves. Meaning?

A good marriage may well be something of a blessed state but, as Jane Austen observed, 'happiness in marriage is entirely a matter of chance'. Yet, as Chaim Bermant also observes, this chance of happiness is 'obviously related to duration, yet we expect to draw our full dividend of bliss almost instantly, and if it fails to materialize we immediately call in the receivers.' His solution is to advocate a lower level of expectations and a higher level of personal responsibility.

And if that fails? Find someone else? Another person? Our selves? The search for love will inevitably continue ...

Appendix:
Methods of Enquiry

1.*The main survey* was produced with the help of *Dateline International*. The data base consisted of over 68,000 members and their response to the *Dateline* questionnaire. The agency itself describes the procedure it followed [10 July, 1990]:

> The statistical report on the Dateline membership file entitled "Mega Stats" was produced from the entire membership file at the time of printing. This sample included all those whose membership had by that stage expired, and any whose membership had been suspended for whatever reason. The member who joined the earliest did so on June 15th, 1975, and incidentally has renewed up until the 7th of September 1990.

> Until recently the membership file was regularly cleared of any members whose membership had expired longer ago than one year, but this practice has ceased (originally to keep the database large for the purposes of the study). The next joining date to the above mentioned member joined on 30th March 1977, and is also a current live member.

> The Mega Stats report was produced from some 68,000 database

records, all of which had been of live members at the time or up to one year before the run date. The way that the numbers were produced was that the records were read and totalled. For the boxes that refer to an "I am" condition this was simple enough, each "I am" incremented the total in the box by one. Where the box referred to an "I want" then the box was incremented if the member had entered a tick ("Yes I do want this in a person"), and was decremented if the member had entered a cross ("No I don't want this"). If the member had left the box blank ("No strong preference"), then the box total was left unchanged. Thus a box with a score of zero could indicate that either the same number of people felt strongly about it on both sides or that nobody at all had any strong feelings. The net score however indicates whether the characteristic is perceived to be a positive or negative one.

Where the member has had to indicate their preference as a range (height and age) then the range has been divided into a number of discrete ranges and the member preferences have incremented all relevant boxes.

2. Subsequently copies of the questionnaire *Relationships in the 1990s*, were sent to over 4000 *ex-Dateline* couples who had indicated they were 'happily settled together'. Replies were received from just over *1000 couples*.

RELATIONSHIPS IN THE 1990s

Because this questionnaire is for statistical purposes only we do not ask you to identify yourself in any way. We do, however, need to connect your questionnaire with that of your partner and for that reason alone could we ask you to consult with your partners about one point only before you seperately fill in these questionnaires - just make up a unique 7 digit number (such as the reverse of your telephone number) and write it in the box below (e.g. 4627867).

The number we have both chosen is [   ]

It is important that you answer the questionnaire on your own. Please do not liaise with your partner.

Although it is not necessary to answer every question, it would be much appreciated if you could attempt all of them.

There are no 'right' or 'wrong' answers; please try to avoid simple 'yes' or 'no' answers and try to express your thoughts and feelings as much as possible. Please elaborate as much as you like, on seperate sheets if necessary.

Even if you don't want us to interview you we would really appreciate your completing this questionnaire.

Your answers are anonymous and strictly confidential.

We first need the following basic information:

Your sex is

Your age is

Your occupation is

Your current income (approx)

Current marital status

MAIN
QUESTIONNAIRE

1. What is the most important part of your current relationship, the reason you want it? Is it love, passion, sexual intimacy, economics, daily companionship or the long-term value of a family relationship? Other?

2. What is the worst thing your partner has ever done to you? What is the worst thing you have done to your parnter?

3. In your relationship is it easy to talk? Who talks more? Would you like more intimate talk - about feelings, problems, the future?

4. Is the kind of love you are giving and receiving now the kind you most want? Have you seen another type in a friend's relationship or a film or a novel that you would find more satisfying?

5. Which is more important: Your job? Your love relationship? Your children? Yourself, having time for yourself?

6. Are you jealous? Of friendships? Career? Other men/women?

7. How similar are you to each other? Have you the same outlook on life?

8. How much do you think your partner loves you?

9. How similar (or different) do you think your current partner is from what you initially requested from Dateline?

10. In choosing a partner and making a relationship work, how important do you consider - compared to

each other - the following? Physical attraction/sex: Personality; Interests/values; 'Character' (like beng 'considerate', for example).

11. Do you consider it normal to be either in love with or desire sex with someone of the same sex?

12. Does AIDS concern you? Have you changed your views about sex since the AIDS epidemic? Have you/will you change your sexual behaviour since the AIDS epidemic?

13. How sympathetic is you partner when you are anxious or under-pressure?

14. How jealous are you of your partner's past relationships?

15. To what degree is the housework shared in your home?

16. How close do you feel to your partner?

17. Do you take much trouble over your appearance?

18. Even in these early stages, have you ever asked for outside help with your relationship?

19. Do you think your partner knows what you really think and feel?

20. Do you hold hands?

21. Do you ever wish your partner was more sexually responsive to you?

22. Do you ever feel 'tied down' by your relationship?

23. How often does your partner make you laugh?

24. How important do you think the sexual side of a realtionship is?

25. Do you tend to express your feelings or hold them in?

26. Would you say your parents had/have a happy marriage?

27. Do you think your partner finds other women/men attractive?

28. Does your love for your partner grow?

29. Do you have children? Are they your own children? Adopted by you? Step child? From this relationship? Living with you now? Their ages:

30. Is your partner dependable in a crisis?

31. How often do you have a serious row?

32. Is there any way in which your partner's work gets in the way of your relationship?

33. Does your relationship remind you much of your parent's marriage?

34. Even in these early stages have you ever separated for a while? For how long?

35. What was the biggest emotional upset you have ever had to face?

36. What do you want most in life?

37. As a child, were you close to your mother? Your father? Did they love you? What did you like most and least about them?

38. How did you feel when you started dating? When you first kissed? First had sex? Did you discuss any of this with your parents? Friends?

39. Are you 'in love' now? How can you tell? How would you define love?

40. What do you think the difference is between being 'in love' and loving someone?

41. How often have you cried yourself to sleep because of problems with someone you loved? Why did you do so? Have you ever contemplated suicide in such situations?

42. At what time in your life have you been the loneliest?

43. How would you describe being in love? The good things, the bad things?

44. How important do you think money is in relationships? Is it a problem for you at all?

45. Who would you say is the cleverer - you or your parnter?

46. Do you often have conflicting views about your partner?

47. What reasons would you give for you and your partner's compatibility?

48. Were you always certain that one day you would meet your 'perfect partner'?

49. Have you a history of repeatedly picking the 'wrong' man/woman?

If applicable: 50. If you have suffered a previous and painful break-up of a relationship: what was the cause? What was the worst thing about the break-up? What helped you get over it?

51. How would you describe both the advantages and disadvantages of being 'single'?

52. How soon did you and your current partner have sexual relations after you first met?

53. Do you think you might now feel 'lost' without your partner?

54. Do you think your partner is attractive to other people?

55. Did you embark on this relationship, at all, in order to get away from your parents?

56. Do you see marriage as an important public commitment?

57. How often do you want to physically touch your partner?

58. Are you ever simply too busy to talk to your partner?

59. In what ways has your partner changed since you met?

60. Do you ever look for (and find) sexual fulfilment outside your relationship?

61. Do you think your partner pays enough attention to his/her appearance?

62. Does your partner help you to choose your clothes?

63. Do you think your expectations about long-term relationships were, and are, 'realistic'?

64. Do you think your partner would understand if you were unfaithful?

65. How much time would you say you spend just with each other?

66. Do you consider there to be enough privacy in relationships (and family life)?

67. When you and your partner disagree, do you tend ot hide it form other people?

68. Do you respect your partner? Do they respect you?

69. Would you say in any sense that children 'hold a marriage together'?

70. To what extent does your relationship have a romantic side?

71. Would you say you were basically happy with your current role in life?

72. Have you ever had sex against your will?

73. Do you think marriage/relationships can suffer when the children eventually leave home?

74. Do you have any strong moral or religious beliefs about marriage?

75. How far do you agree on who does what in your relationship?

76. Do you think your partner is totally honest with themselves?

77. Is your partner kind to you?

78. Would you say you find sexual fulfilment in your current relationship?

79. Do you get on well with your in-laws?

80. Do you generally expect your current relationship to 'last forever'?

81. Would you say your partner is proud of you? Are you proud of him/her?

82. Apart from work, does your partner go out without you often?

83. Did you settle with your current partner in any way for financial reasons?

84. Would you say it was 'love at first sight'?

85. Have you as many children as you would like?

86. How close is your partner to the children?

87. Do you and your partner basically agree about how the children should be brought up?

88. Do you often just hug your children?

90. Do you ever look after the children on your own?

91. Do you ever feel that your children rule your life?

92. Do you always approve of the way in which your parnter behaves with the children?

93. How often do the children get on your 'nerves'?

94. When (and how often) are your problems due to your partner's behaviour/feelings?

95. How sexually experienced were you before you met your current partner?

96. How would your summarize your current sexual relationship as compared with your previous ones?

97. Does your partner ever 'get on your nerves'?

98. When you disagree with your partner, who tends to give in?

99. Do you find your partner attractive?

100. How important is companionship in your marriage?

101. How fortunate do you think you were to meet your current partner?

102. If there were serious problems in your relationship could you go to your family for help?

103. Have you ever been attracted to people of the same sex as you?

104. Has your partner many irritating habits?

105. Do you think it is silly to stay in a relationship 'for the sake of the children'?

106. Does your partner ever embarrass you in public? How much?

107. Do you think you ever take your partner for granted?

108. If you are unhappy, can you easily discuss it with your partner?

109. What are your feelings concerning divorce? For example do you consider it wrong?

110. Are you concerned about your partner's physical appearance, and clothing?

111. Do you think you understand your partner very well?

112. Would you describe your present relationship as 'successful'?

113. Do you think your partner feels possessive about you?

114. Would you call yourself happy?

115. In your current relationship who tends to make the important decisions?

116. Would you call yourself a feminist, or (if male) a supporter of feminism?

117. Do you like to feel that you are dependent on your partner, or independent, or interdependent - both of your lives being entwined?

118. Could you describe how you think 'love' has changed you?

119. Do you think there are definite phases in love? For example do you think there is an early exciting/idyllic phase which will almost certainly wear off in time?

120. Thinking of partners/relationships you had before your present one, would you summarize the ways in which the present one is different?

121. Do you think sex gets less important as you get older?

122. Do you ever feel you have 'unhealthy' needs and cravings for love and affection?

123. Have you ever felt that you were 'owned' or suffocated, held down, in a relationship, so that you wanted out?

124. Have you ever had a nagging fear of losing someone else's love, or being deserted? That the other person would grow tired of you?

125. How do you feel if someone is very emotionally dependent on you in a relationship? Needs you more? Complains that you don't love them enough?

126. Do you think men take love and falling in love as seriously as women do?

127. Does your partner see you as an equal? Or are there times when you feel you are being treated as an inferior?

128. What is the best thing about sex with you partner? The worst?

129. When do you feel most passionate? How does it feel?

130. In sex do you usually like to be more passive or active (dominant)?

131. To what degree do you discuss your day to day concerns with your partner?

132. How similar is your current partner to the man/woman 'of your dreams'?

133. Do you ever feel lonely?

134. Do you enjoy, at all, sexy books or videos?

135. How well do you think your partner knows your friends?

136. To what extent does your partner 'nag' you?

137. Do you worry much about your partner being unfaithful?

138. Does your partner support you in whatever you try to do?

139. To what extent did your parents play a part in choosing your current partner?

140. How many people did you seriously go out with before your current partner?

141. Is your partner ever truly 'nasty' to you?

142. Do you see much of your family? Did you used to see more of them before you met your current parnter?

143. Do you think your partner puts you before the children?

144. Do you tend to go along with what your children want?

145. Do most of your friends have children?

146. Would you say your partner is a 'good' mother/father?

147. How has your general outlook on life changed since you had children?

148. Do you often have rows in front of the children?

149. Would you say you are 'close' to your children?

150. How often are you children 'too much' for you?

151. Would you say your children bring you happiness?

152. Do you like being with your children?

153. How often does your partner lose his/her temper with the children?

154. Would you say you are a 'good' parent?

155. Are your children happy?

156. If you have no children, please answer this question: Why haven't you had any children?

157. How possessive do you feel about your partner?

158. If you have been married before (or been in a serious long-term relationship), does it cause problems with your current partner?

159. Try and describe how you think you might react/feel if your partner suddenly left you.

160. In trouble can you rely on one or two good friends (other than your partner)?

161. How much do you miss your partner when you are apart?

162. Who is usually the first to 'make up' after a row?

163. Do you ever feel pressured into sex? Into liking sex?

164. Do you use birth control? What kind? What are its advantages and disadvantages?

165. Have you ever had an abortion? Why did you decide to have it? How did you feel after you had it?

166. For Females: What is or has been the most important relationship with a woman in your life? Describe the woman you have loved the most. Hated the most.

167. For Males: What is or has been the most important relationship with a man in your life?

Describe the man you have loved the most. Hated the most.

168. For Females: What do you like about your closest woman friend?

169. For Males: What do you like about your closest male friend?

170. Have any feelings about feminism/the 'women's movement' and have its ideas affected your life?

171. How do you feel about getting older?

172. What do you think is the biggest problem in society today?

173. Who are the two living individuals you admire the most - male and female?

174. Thinking of characters in a film, in history, or in a novel, how would you like to see you and your partner's relationship? (e.g. Romeo and Juliet, 'Harry and Sally' etc).

Now that you have completed this questionnaire post it to us in the envelope provided - no stamp is necessary.

Thank you very much for your help.

Acknowledgments:

Introduction

Patrick Carnes (1989) *Out of the Shadows: Understanding Sexual Attraction*, Basic Books: New York.

Stefan Mehlisch (1989) 'Mate selection', Unpublished paper.

Chapter One

Rudyard Kipling (orig. 1890) 'The widower', in *Rudyard Kipling's Verse: Definitive Edition*, Doubleday: New York.

Robin Norwood (1986) *Women Who Love Too Much*, Arrow Books: London.

Meredith Tax (1990) *Passionate Women*, Virago: London.

Chapter Three

HMSO (1990) *Social Trends 20: 1990 Edition*, HMSO: London.

Chapter Six

Department of Health, the Welsh Office (1988) *Short-term Prediction of HIV Infection and AIDS in England and Wales; Report of a Working Group* (aka, 'Cox Report') HMSO: London.

John Haskey (1988) 'Trends in marriage and divorce, and cohort analyses of the proportions of marriages ending in divorce', pp. 21-28, *Population Trends*, 54, Winter 1988, OPCS:HMSO.

HMSO (1990) *Social Trends 20: 1990 Edition*, HMSO: London.

A. Mariotto (1988) 'Rate of growth of AIDS epidemic in Europe: a comparative analysis,' pp. 63-64, appendix 9, in the 'Cox Report.'

John Naisbitt and Patricia Aburdene (1990) *Mega-Trends 2000*, Sidgwick and Jackson: London.

Tom W. Smith (1990) 'Adult Sexual Behaviour in 1989: Number of Partners, Frequency, and Risk', GSS Topical Report No.18, paper presented to the American Association for the Advancement of Science, February 1990, New Orleans.

WHO Report, reported in *Guardian*, 22 June, 1990, p.24

Malcolm Wicks and Kathleen Kiernan (1990) *Family Changes*, Family Policy Studies Centre: London.

Chapter Seven

Martin S.Bergmann (1987) *The Anatomy of Loving*, Columbia University Press: New York.

Anthony Clare (1990) 'Wedded Bliss - Is it a Myth?' *The Sunday Times*, 4 March, 1990.

Erich Fromm (1975) *The Art of Loving*, George Allen and Unwin:London.

Bob Mullan (1984) *The Mating Trade*, Routledge and Kegan Paul: London

Ethel Spector Person (1990) *Love and Fateful Encounters*, Bloomsbury: London.

Woman's Own (1990), 26 June, 1990.

Chapter Eight

Peter Cannon (1990) 'Wife Shopping', pp.8-10 *The Listener*, 5 July 1990

Suzanne Gordon (1976) *Lonely in America*, Simon and Schuster: London.

James J. Lynch (1977) *The Broken Heart*, Basic Books: New York.

Bob Mullan (1984) *Perfect Partners?*, Boxtree: London.

Helge Rubenstein (ed) (1990) *The Oxford Book of Marriage*, Oxford University Press: Oxford.

Conclusions

Chaim Bermant (1990) 'Marriage á la mode in the nineties,' *Observer*, 24 June, 1990.

Francesca M. Cancian (1987) *Love in America*, Cambridge University Press: Cambridge.

Heather Formani (1990) *Men: The Darker Continent*, Heinemann: London

Grey's (1990) 'The New Man', June 1990.

Brigid Hulson and Robin Russel (1990) 'Psychological foundations of couple relationships,' unpublished paper (to appear in *Handbook of Couples Therapy in Britain*, eds. Hooper and Dryden).

Annette Lawson (1989) *Adultery*, Basil Blackwell: Oxford.

Anthony Storr (1988) *The School of Genius*, Andre Deutsch: London.

Donald W. Winnicott (1969) 'The Capacity To Be Alone', in *The Maturational Process and the Faciliating Environment*